D0444193

Re-Imagine the World

Re-Imagine the World

An Introduction to the Parables of Jesus

BERNARD BRANDON SCOTT

Polebridge Press

Published in 2001 by Polebridge Press, P. O. Box 6144, Santa Rosa, California, 95406.

Library of Congress Cataloging-in-Publication Data

Scott, Bernard Brandon, 1941—
    Re-imagine the World : an introduction to the parables of Jesus / Bernard Brandon Scott.
    p. cm.
    Includes bibliographical references (p.) and index.
    ISBN 0-944344-86-0
    1. Jesus Christ-- Parables. I. Title: Reimagine the world. II. Title.

BT375.3 .S36 2001
226.8'06--dc21

2001054860

For Chester Cadieux
"Be the Best"

&

My colleagues at
Phillips Theological Seminary

Contents

Cameo Essays & Texts

Acknowledgments

In Robert Funk's seminar at Vanderbilt University many years ago I first got a glimpse of the parables' power. It gives me great honor to have this book published by Polebridge, his press. My intellectual debts to him are immense.

I want to thank my colleagues at Phillips Theological Seminary for all the fine conversation and support they have offered me. Some have even taken my work so seriously as to try to figure out what it might mean for their disciplines. No higher compliment can be paid. The school's president, William Tabbernee, has set a high standard in both leadership and scholarship. Chester Cadieux has been of one those benefactors who has supported the best values of the institution. Many thanks to all who made PTS a great place.

Char Matejovsky of Polebridge has prodded and supported me, two things an author always needs. Tom Hall has provided an expert proof-reader's eye. His effort has much improved the book.

Margaret Lee has made it possible for me to re-imagine life. I tremble to think what life would be without her.

1

The Parables
and Jesus

The parables of Jesus, which rank among the supreme literary creations of western literature, testify to the consummate religious genius who had a unique vision of God, a vision he discovered and communicated in parables.

Those parables have remained riddles or mysteries almost from the very beginning. Mark seems to represent the position of many. "To you has been given the secret of the kingdom of God, but for those outside, everything comes in parables" (Mark 4:11, NRSV). For Mark a parable is a riddle. This saying in Mark indicates that from a very early time Jesus' parables have mystified. Allegory has trod this path sorting out those on the inside who understand from those on the outside who don't.

Yet for many others, the parables are simple stories, illustrations for the common people. Such interpreters almost always end up with trite meanings for the parables or import the meaning from elsewhere.

I have never found Jesus' parables simple. The arrogance of modernity sees the ancients as simple and ourselves as complex and sophisticated. Yet Homer, an oral poet who could neither read nor write, composed two of the greatest poems of all times.

How do we know Jesus?

The focus of this book is on Jesus' parables. By Jesus I mean the historical Jesus — the Galilean, Jewish peasant as reconstructed by the tools of historical criticism. I am trying to understand what Jesus intended by the parables. This focus does not deny the importance or legitimacy of studies that deal only with the parables as they appear in the gospels. My focus is elsewhere, on the historical Jesus.

Some complain that this enterprise is too hypothetical, but all interpretation is hypothetical. We construct hypotheses to try to explain the material, the texts that we have. Even the very Greek New Testament we work with is a hypothetical construct, since we do not posses the original manuscripts. It is a scholarly reconstruction. Translations are even more hypothetical and tendentious, making assumptions about equivalences in different languages. I have become very suspicious of translations. Dates for the gospels are hypothetical, as is any notion of the background of a given gospel or the context in

Jesus Seminar

The Jesus Seminar was organized under the auspices of the Westar Institute to renew the quest of the historical Jesus and to report the results of its research to the general public. At its inception in 1985, thirty scholars took up the challenge. Eventually more than two hundred professionally trained specialists, called Fellows, joined the group. The Seminar met twice a year to debate technical papers that had been prepared and circulated in advance. At the close of debate on each agenda item, Fellows of the Seminar voted.

The first step in the work of the Jesus Seminar was to inventory and classify all the words attributed to Jesus in the first three centuries of the common era. The inventory covers all the surviving gospels and reports from the period, not just the canonical gospels.

The goal of the Seminar was to review each of the fifteen hundred items in the inventory and determine which of them could be ascribed with a high degree of probability to Jesus. But the interpretation of the data was to be excluded from the agenda of the Seminar and left to individual scholars working from their own perspectives.

The model of the red letter editions of the gospels suggested that the Seminar should adopt one of two options in its votes: either Jesus said it or he did not say it. A vote recognizing the words as authentic would entail printing the items in red; a vote recognizing the words as inauthentic meant that they would be left in regular black print.

Scholars do not like simple choices. As a compromise the Seminar adopted four categories: red, pink, gray, and black. Fellows were per-

which it was written. We are caught in a web of hypotheses from which we cannot escape, so surely a few more cannot hurt.

There are in this book no arguments about which parables actually go back to Jesus. I accept for the most part the votes of the Jesus Seminar. I was a charter member of the Seminar, participated actively in the debates about the parables and was a co-author of the first report of the Jesus Seminar on the parables. Where I disagree with the decisions of the Seminar I will so indicate.

I have often admired how auditors give in percentages their level of confidence in their report. They do this because they recognize that their reports are hypothetical too. Their data, their numbers are dependent on others.

---

mitted to cast ballots under two different options for understanding the four colors.

Option 1
  red: I would include this item unequivocally in the database for determining who Jesus was.
  pink: I would include this item with reservations (or modifications) in the database.
  gray: I would not include this item in the database, but I might make use of some of the content in determining who Jesus was.
  black: I would not include this item in the primary database.

Option 2
  red: Jesus undoubtedly said this or something very like it.
  pink: Jesus probably said something like this.
  gray: Jesus did not say this, but the ideas contained in it are close to his own.
  black: Jesus did not say this; it represents the perspective or content of a later or different tradition.

The results of the Seminar's debates and voting were published in two volumes: *The Five Gospels: What Did Jesus Really Say?* and *The Acts of Jesus: What Did Jesus Really Do?* The significance of the title *Five Gospels* is that the Gospel of Thomas is included as an equal, for historical purposes, of the four Canonical Gospels. Besides printing the sayings and deeds in the appropriate color determined by the voting, there is also a fresh, new translation (The Scholars Version) and a commentary explaining the votes on each saying or deed.

Scholars might follow the example of auditors and indicate their confidence in their hypotheses and arguments. The Jesus Seminar did just this when it published its reports in colors indicating a range from high confidence to no confidence. I have tried to indicate where I am highly confident of my arguments and where I am guessing. Let the reader beware.

To my mind the two strongest arguments for the authenticity of the parable tradition are the rarity of parables in the Christian tradition and the coherence of the themes of the parables. Parables only occur in the Synoptic Gospels (Matthew, Mark, Luke) and the Gospel of Thomas. No parables are ever placed on the lips of Jesus' opponents, nor does Paul or any other New Testament author use or create parables. The Gospel of John contains no parables. In the later Christian tradition, many different sayings of Jesus are reported, but no new parables. The narrowness of the tradition impresses me and appears to point to one source.

When we examine all the parables as a corpus they cohere, they make sense as a group. One of the burdens of this book is to indicate this coherence. We find in the parables phrases and words that are clearly the hand of an evangelist. In this regard the parables of the Gospel of Thomas seem to me to exhibit about the same degree of editing as those of the other gospel writers. That is what I would

---

Gospel of Thomas

The Gospel of Thomas is a new and important source for the sayings and parables of Jesus. It contains one hundred fourteen sayings and parables but lacks a narrative framework.

Thomas has survived in complete form only in a Coptic translation found among the fifty-two tractates that make up the Coptic Gnostic Library discovered at Nag Hammadi, Egypt, in 1945. Fragments of three Greek versions of Thomas were discovered at Oxyrhynchus, Egypt, about 1900 C.E. The Greek fragments can be dated by the style of writing to about 200 C.E. The first edition of Thomas was probably composed during the decade 50–60 C.E.

Thomas is widely regarded as an independent witness to the sayings of Jesus, comparable in form to Q, a hypothetical sayings collection believed to have functioned as one of the two sources utilized by Matthew and Luke in creating their gospels.

For a translation of the Gospel of Thomas see MILLER, *The Complete Gospels*.

expect. After a while, the editing style of each evangelist becomes easy to spot. Well, maybe not so easy nor always so clear, yet patterns begin to emerge. None of the gospel writers was a stenographer interested in preserving the exact words of Jesus. They retell the parables in their own way, just as we would expect.

Adolf Jülicher, the founder of modern parable interpretation, demonstrated the often ill and awkward fit of the parable to its gospel context. Thus it becomes clear that most parables existed prior to their incorporation into a gospel.

While I harbor no illusions about being able to recover the very words of Jesus, I am convinced that we have the feel of Jesus' parables, their form and texture, if not their exact wording.

Modest proposal

When we seek to understand Jesus' parables what are we doing? What is our goal? Some seek to understand the mind of Jesus. We often view reading as entering the author's mind. We imagine we are engaging in conversation with the author. But the author is absent and silent. When we read, we bring the story to life. We become in some sense a co-author of the text. The conversation takes place in our brain. The text is just letters, silent letters, until we read those letters and give them voice, life, and imagination.

Or we could study the parables to construct a life of Jesus. But there are several problems with this proposal, as well.

- The parables are not autobiographical. They are fictions told by the storyteller. We do not know how they relate to his biography.
- We do not have sufficient data for a biography of Jesus. We do not know the outline of his life. We know he was born but not when or where. We know he died under Pontius Pilate but not when and not exactly why. We know some of the events between his birth and death, but not how to arrange them. What outline we have of a life of Jesus comes from whoever wrote the Gospel according to Mark, probably sometime after the destruction of the Jerusalem Temple in 70 CE. Mark had no more access to evidence for an outline of Jesus' life than do we. So we are left with no way to arrange the material in chronological order, no way to see development, whether psychological or any other kind.

What can we do? The parables give us access to the way Jesus re-imagined the possibility of living, of being in the world. They are not just religious, not just about God, although they are that too. As we investigate the parables as fictions we will begin to see that they are multifaceted re-imaginings of life, of the possibilities of life. They help us imagine how we might live life in this world. To say more now would be to anticipate what we must discover.

The famous literary scholar Harold Bloom observed that from Shakespeare's plays we learn little or nothing about Shakespeare, "but if you give many years to reading him incessantly, you begin to know what he is not" (p. 51). While we know considerably more about Shakespeare's life than we do about Jesus', the plays are not a source for Shakespeare's life. Similarly for Jesus; his parables are not a source from which we will find out much about Jesus' life. Jesus is not a topic of Jesus' parables.

For Bloom the wonder of Shakespeare's plays is what he terms "the invention of the human." Bloom sees in Shakespeare's creation of Hamlet the first modern consciousness. For him, Freud, who was deeply interested in Shakespeare, did not have an Oedipus complex, but a Hamlet complex. Whether Bloom is correct in his audacious interpretation of Shakespeare is irrelevant. But it does suggest that what we finally learn from Jesus' parables is how life can be imagined.

There are always those who think that Shakespeare's plays could not have been written by Shakespeare, because Shakespeare is deemed too lower class, too uneducated, etc., to have produced such great works. Even by the testimony of his contemporaries he was an ordinary sort of person, someone with whom you could have a drink. He was good natured and unassuming. He does seem to have had an instinct for business. Could someone so ordinary have written these great plays? Almost inevitably those who challenge Shakespeare's authorship prefer a lord or count as the author.

In the case of Jesus the countermove is to maintain that the parables are simple. But this is to miss their depth, elegance, and subtlety. At times critics have complained that my interpretations of the parables are too complex or subtle. If Jesus' parables are so complex or subtle, the simple folk who comprised Jesus' audience could not have understood them. But the apparent complexity is on our part. Because we do not share the cultural world of Jesus and his audience, their repertoire of social and cultural values, literary and story types, the interpreter must make evident what would have been assumed, obvious, or intuitive to Jesus' audience. Modern interpretations of Shakespeare's plays make it look as if the average Elizabethan could never understand the plays. Yet they did, and Shakespeare was a very popular and successful playwright.

Assumptions about Jesus

I make a number of assumptions about the historical Jesus. These assumptions are not what I start with, the *a priori* assumptions from which I deduce the evidence. No, they are really the conclusions of years of working with the evidence, of trying to understand it, of using a variety of methods to make sense of it. This list is by no means complete, and you will doubtless think of many items I should have added.

Jesus was a Galilean, Jewish peasant. For me, each of these three words is important, for each helps define the context in which Jesus is to be understood.

Galilean

The archaeology of Galilee has led scholars to re-evaluate the social and cultural situation of Jesus. Three facts are important.
- Galilee had a significant gentile, Greek speaking population. Jesus lived in Nazareth, a small Israelite town, which was about three miles distant from the large Hellenistic city Sepphoris.
- Farming in Galilee was rapidly becoming commercialized. Small farms were being replaced by large estates. Many people were dislocated and the work force became more specialized.
- The Judaism of Galilee was not identical to that of Judea and was probably viewed by Judeans with suspicion. Judaism was not long established in Galilee and Judaism as practiced in Galilean villages was certainly quite different from the that of the elites of Jerusalem. The Temple was remote, probably suspect, and viewed as a drain upon the local area.

Jewish

Jesus was Jewish and had no intention of being anything else. He viewed himself as loyal to the traditions of Israel. His was one of many competing voices at the time attempting to articulate the meaning of the tradition of Abraham and Moses. He would have been very surprised at the development of Christianity.

Jesus stands in the long and continuing tradition of Jewish story-telling. He works with a traditional repertoire of tales.

Peasant

Peasant describes his social class. He comes from the bottom of society. He is landless. At some point his family has lost its land, probably to one of the growing estates in Galilee. As a carpenter we should not imagine him as part of an artisan lower middle class. He is a day laborer. He belongs to what anthropologists refer to as the disposables. Since carpenters frequently built scaffolding for stone work, perhaps he was employed in the construction work ongoing in Sepphoris, which Herod Antipas was rebuilding.

There is no credible evidence that Jesus could read and write. The story in Luke 4 of Jesus reading in the Synagogue in Nazareth is Luke's fabrication. He imagines Jesus as like himself, able to read and write. The story printed in the Gospel of John of Jesus writing in the sand (John 8:53–9:11) only implies that he was making marks in the sand with a stick, not writing names in the sand. Furthermore, the story is not historical, does not belong to the Gospel of John, and occurs late in the manuscript tradition.

Jesus was an oral storyteller or oral poet. Oral folks think differently than literate folks. As the great student of orality, Walter Ong, noted, in an oral world "you must think memorable thoughts" (p. 34). For our purposes the greatest difference between oral folks and us literates is that they think concretely, we think abstractly. Concrete thinking is not a substitute for abstract thought; it is a different way of thinking. Jesus thinks in parable. To ask him what they mean, what is their point, would appear to him nonsensical. They have no point, they are the point. If you had challenged Jesus' parable, he would not have explained it, but told you a different parable. The differences between orality and literacy will plague us at every turn and seriously hinder our efforts to understand the parables.

Jesus did not intend to found a religion

This is really a restatement of the point that he was Jewish, but it needs to be re-emphasized because of the contrary assumption from which the parables have so often been interpreted.

Yet the parables created a re-imagined world in which belief in Jesus' vindication made sense. But that is the topic for another book.

I find it difficult to state in a positive fashion just what Jesus was about. I don't see the evidence that he had a clear program. He was probably not a reformer. He was a storyteller with a different take on the tradition of Israel. He had a vision of how life might be, ought to be.

Jesus was crucified under Pontius Pilate

This is important for several reasons.

- He ultimately came into conflict with the Roman Empire. The Empire bears ultimate responsibility for his death. I assume that conflict was real, not imagined.
- Jesus was a conflictive personality. He made people angry, angry enough to think his death was a good idea. A quiet, pietistic Jesus will not do.
- Crucifixion points out who held ultimate power in the first century — Rome. Its presence is always there, whether implicit or explicit.

What Language the Parables?

The parables of Jesus are preserved in Greek and those in the Gospel of Thomas in Coptic, although clearly the latter were translated from the Greek. Since Jesus was a Galilean peasant and spoke Aramaic, the common assumption is that Jesus originally spoke the parables in Aramaic. But if they were translated from Aramaic, the Greek is remarkably free of Aramaic idioms. It may be the tradition was bilingual from the beginning. Several factors point in this direction:

- There were many Greek-speakers in Galilee and Nazareth is only three and one half miles distant from Sepphoris, a large Greek-speaking city.
- As a *tekton* (builder) Jesus would likely have worked in Sepphoris and so would have acquired some Greek.
- The hypothetical source Q is generally thought to have been composed by village scribes in Greek in Galilee before 70CE.
- Peter, at least, was present in Antioch and other cities of the Empire. He almost certainly spoke Greek.

I do not think the parables explain why Jesus was crucified. We probably lack the evidence for a clear explanation of the motives for the crucifixion. But the interpretation of the parables must explain why people would have thought Jesus was dangerous, perhaps even in league with Satan.

Last minute thoughts

Twenty-three of thirty-five parables ascribed to Jesus received a red or pink vote by the Jesus Seminar. Since this book is an introduction to the parables, a selection process was necessary. I had two principal goals in mind.

Each parable must receive an independent analysis, so that we, I as author and you as reader, will have sufficient time to examine each parable. Parables are like jewels: they are best appreciated from a variety of points of view. Lying jumbled together in a box it's hard to appreciate their individual beauty.

Our analysis of the parables should contribute to a profile of Jesus. The study of each parable should not be just seriatim but become cumulative in its impact.

My selection criteria were subjective. I picked those parables that had been most formative in my own thought, represented the different types (one-liners and narrative parables), and were preserved in the various layers of the tradition, e.g., Q, Thomas, and the synoptic gospels.

Following the analysis of the individual parables, two chapters are devoted to putting it all together, to asking, "What does it add up to?" Chapter 12, "Re-imagining the World," indicates how for me the parables imply a profile of Jesus. Chapter 13, "Living in a Re-imagined World," is my effort to answer the question, "what do the parables mean today?" I have chosen to do that in a somewhat autobiographical fashion.

This book contains little of the superstructure of scholarship, although I hope that does not mean that it is not scholarly. A bibliographic essay is included as an appendix and discusses books and essays that have been critical in forming my view on the parables and will serve as a guide to the reader for further study.

I have given myself the freedom to say what I really think without the caution and constraint of footnotes or arguing with other scholars. I have tried to be fair and indicate when I'm speculating. I have written a scholarly commentary on all the parables, *Hear Then the Parable*, where the reader can find fuller documentation for my arguments, although I should warn the reader that on some points I have changed my mind. This book is not just a simple version of my more technical commentary, but a rethinking of the issues.

Parables receiving a Red or Pink Vote

Leaven		
Luke 13:20–21	Red	
Matt 13:33	Red	
Thomas 96	Pink	
Samaritan		
Luke 10:30–35	Red	
Shrewd Manager		
Luke 16:1–8a	Red	
Vineyard Laborers		
Matt 20:1–15	Red	
Mustard Seed		
Thomas 20	Red	
Mark 4:30–32	Pink	
Luke 13:18–19	Pink	
Matt 13:31–32	Pink	
Lost Coin		
Luke 15:8–9	Pink	
Friend at Midnight		
Luke 11:5–8	Pink	
Treasure		
Matt 13:44	Pink	
Thomas 109	Pink	
Lost Sheep		
Luke 15:4–6	Pink	
Matt 18:12–13	Pink	
Thomas 107	Gray	
Corrupt Judge		
Luke 18:2–5	Pink	
Prodigals		
Luke 15:11–32	Pink	
Dinner Party		
Thomas 64	Pink	
Luke 14:16–23	Pink	
Matt 22:2–13	Black	

Pearl	
Thomas 76	Pink
Matt 13:45–46	Pink
The Assassin	
Thomas 98	Pink
Seed & Harvest	
Mark 4:26–29	Pink
Thomas 21	Gray
Unforgiving Slave	
Matt 18:23–34	Pink
Leased Vineyard	
Thomas 65	Pink
Mark 12:1–8	Gray
Matt 21:33–39	Gray
Luke 20:9–15a	Gray
Rich Farmer, Rich Investor	
Thomas 63	Pink
Luke 12:16–20	Pink
Money in Trust	
Luke 19:13, 15–24	Pink
Matt 25:14–28	Pink
Pharisee and Toll Collector	
Luke 18:10–14a	Pink
Barren Tree	
Luke 13:6–9	Pink
Sower	
Mark 4:3–8	Pink
Matt 13:3–8	Pink
Thomas 9	Pink
Luke 8:5–8a	Pink
Empty Jar	
Thomas 97	Pink

I have tried to imagine with the parables. Like the ancient rabbis, I think that parables demand imagination, and so occasionally I have given mine free rein.

At some points I will comment on the Greek text. This is unavoidable because no translation is ever adequate. Some things simply cannot be translated. I will sometimes offer my own translation, or point out a range of meaning hard to translate, and then again will attempt to arrange a translation so that you can get a feel for the Greek behind the translation.

The translations of the gospels are those of the *Scholars Version* (*The Complete Gospels*) and the other Scriptures are from the NRSV. I have arranged each parable into "sound lines" which attempt to give you a visual picture of the rhythm and pattern which the ancients heard. Try reading them out loud like poetry and begin to appreciate their careful craft.

When I refer to ancient texts, you can find the translations I used listed in "Works Cited" at the end of the book. Likewise, when I refer to modern authors in the text, you will find the complete bibliographic citation in "Works Cited."

2

On Parables

In his parables Jesus re-imagined a world in which to live. And through them his followers learned to live in a re-imagined world. Furthermore, they are our only means of access to that world. He called it the kingdom of God. How can parables re-imagine a world?

Parables belong to the wisdom tradition and so are related to proverbs and aphorisms. Actually, in Hebrew the same world, *mashal*, stands for all three. But parables differ from proverbs and aphorisms in that they consist of short narrative fictions that serve as metaphors. This way of employing fiction gives the parable a distinctive quality: it is not really about what it seems to be about. Its real subject is disguised and can be discerned only through insight.

To discover how the parables of Jesus function, we shall follow three inter-related trails:

- Myth and parable
- Uncommon themes from common wisdom
- The parable as metaphor

Myth and parable

A parable is a short narrative fiction. To properly interpret a parable, we must pay careful attention to the story — its plot and characters, the way it tells its story. The power of story is its ability to release and empower the imagination. In story we can re-imagine the world, we can be other than we normally are. But stories can work

13

Parable in Greek and Hebrew

The English word "Parable" is a transliteration (letter for letter) of the Greek word *parabole*. The Greek word has two parts. *Para* means "beside" and *ballein* means "to throw." *Parabole* in Greek is something "thrown beside" something else, that is, a comparison. The Hebrew word translated by the Greek *parabole* is *mashal* (plural, *meshalim*), whose primary meaning is "proverb" and it has a wide extension of meanings in the Hebrew Bible. In the Hebrew Bible there are no parables like the short narrative fictions of Jesus and the rabbis.

in one of two ways — they can either support the world as defined and perceived by the dominant culture, or they can subvert that world. The maintenance of the status quo is the function of myth; Jesus' parables belong to the latter type of story.

Myth has a passion for order; it gives the chaos of our daily lives a manageable form by resolving the irreconcilable into a story that makes sense of the conflicts.

An example may help make this clearer. American society operates with a fundamental tension between our belief that all people are created equal and the evident fact that they are not. The Horatio Alger cycle of stories resolves this opposition. The Alger hero, by honesty, cheerful perseverance, and hard work, achieves a just reward. The hero's poor state at the beginning of the story is equivalent to the inequality in society; his final wealth reflects the ideal of our all being created equal. His hard work is the narrative bridge by which he moves from lack of wealth to wealth. Thus the opposition between reality and belief is resolved by narrative. Inequality in society is due not to some fundamental error in society's belief system but in the individual who fails to work. This popular myth is at the root of America's long term problem with welfare programs.

The power of myth, as Lévi-Strauss observed, is that "myths operate in men's minds without their being aware of the fact" (p. 12). Because we are unaware of the operation of myth, it can subtly convince us that fundamental conflicts are resolvable. When myths are exposed as myths, as conflicts that have no resolution, the result is very painful. The loss of a cherished myth makes us feel alone in the world, abandoned — just as many felt when the destruction of the World Trade Center annihilated the illusion of America's invulnerability. But it also offers the chance to re-imagine our situation in the world.

Because myth is so very powerful, so effective in easing the pain of irresolvable conflict, it often overwhelms the efforts of those who seek to expose it. Three famous examples may help us to see the point. Jane Austen's novels are full of wit and irony that expose the stultifying effects of English class structure and the precarious role of women in Regency England. Yet later readers of Austen often miss the irony and take the novels as nostalgic romances, even though she is clearly anti-romantic. Similarly Mark Twain's *Huckleberry Finn* is an attack on American race relations. Yet today it is often read as a portrait of innocent life in rural nineteenth century America, or condemned and banned because of its image of Jim, the escaped slave. In more recent times, Larry McMurtry wrote *Lonesome Dove* as a corrective to the American myth of the wild west, but it has become an icon of that very myth. Myth can often rewrite the very story that seeks to expose it as myth.

Jesus' parables take the other path that is open to story: they re-imagine a world that subverts the status quo. To attack myth, a story must sometimes be outrageous and offensive. When the Samaritan turned out to be the hero, Jesus' Jewish audience was more than surprised. It was outraged at such an offensive notion. And by comparing the kingdom of God to leaven he necessarily violated the religious sensibilities of most, if not all of his hearers. Because parables expose

Where Do Parables Occur?

Parables are not found in the Hebrew Bible; they appear in only three canonical gospels (there are none in the Gospel of John) and the Gospel of Thomas. By far the most common use of the parable is in rabbinic literature. But even here the evidence is late. The *Mishnah* (about 200 CE), the earliest collection of rabbinic material, has only one parable. Not until the writings of the fifth century rabbis do parables become common, and then they occur in a set form in which the parable illustrates the exegesis of Torah. There is no contemporaneous evidence of parable tellers at the time of Jesus. We should probably conclude that Jesus is at the beginning of the common folk tradition of the parable and for that reason his parables are not as stereotyped in form as those of the later rabbis.

myths as false answers to life's hard realities, they also expose their audiences to discomfort and pain. We no longer take offense at the parables, because myth has reclaimed the parables for us, and we no longer experience their assault on myth and their re-imagining of life apart from myth. We must pay attention to the parables' stories and understand them in their historical, cultural context in order to experience anew the way they shook the cultural foundations of Jesus' world.

A parable's narrative is a way of thinking, a way not inferior to but different from abstract thought. Therefore, since the logic of parable is different from the logic of abstract thought, reducing the parable's narrative to an abstract point thwarts its purpose and forfeits its meaning. Instead we must learn to hear the story. The crux is in the concrete particular, not the abstract generalization.

Uncommon themes from common wisdom

One of the distinctive ways Jesus subverts the mythical world is by employing minor themes from the tradition of Israel. Operating with a minor theme allows him to play with the less known and so surprise an audience. The most obvious example of a minor theme, although it is not usually noticed as one, is the governing symbol of Jesus' language, the kingdom of God. This was a relatively infrequent term in the first century. The more dominant themes such as the day of the Lord, or God as king, or even Torah, are absent from Jesus' parables.

This preference for minor themes appears also in the parables. The Rich Farmer draws on a common theme concerning greed, a major problem in a limited-goods society like first-century Palestine. Since in that world wealth is finite, what the rich man hoards is not available for distribution. Greed, then, is a denial of community. The Thomas version of this parable, The Rich Investor, represents the major theme: the rich man of that parable uses his money to make more money. Since Thomas takes a negative view of merchants, this is not surprising. The voice of the Thomas parable is common wisdom. But the version in Luke differs. There the problem is not the accumulation of wealth (greed) but its disposal, or rather the lack of disposal. This represents a very minor theme in the tradition and discloses a distinctive voice.

The Prodigals invokes the traditional theme of two sons, one elder and the other younger, with the sons playing stereotyped roles. The elder son, usually loyal and upright, is rejected in favor of the younger son, usually cast in the role of a rogue. (In mythic form, this motif was used by Israel for its own self-identification.) At the conclusion of Jesus' parable, when an audience expects the father to reject the elder son for protesting the younger son's reception, the father instead responds, "My child, you are always at my side. Everything that's mine is yours" — a profound shock to the audience's expectations.

Even in their use of stereotypes the parables play against expectation. The proverbially tiny mustard seed suggests that the parable will develop the theme of smallness. Instead, at the parable's conclusion the incongruous theme of the great cedar of Lebanon appears.

In each of these parables that play against the expectations of common wisdom, a distinctive voice speaks. But that voice is in jeopardy because, even though these parables both come from and play against common wisdom, in the end common wisdom frequently wins. Each of these parables has been reclaimed by common wisdom, either in the process of transmission, as in the case of Thomas' the Rich Investor, or by means of subsequent interpretation. Since The interpretation customarily employs common wisdom, one of the reservoirs of myth, it has often removed the parable's fangs. In each of the above parables the expected wisdom has overwhelmed the parable, so that most people think that the elder brother is punished and the mustard

Types of Parables

Traditionally, scholars have distinguished between two types of parables used by Jesus. Similitudes are parables in which the comparison "like" is expressed. The Leaven is an example of a similitude. The other type of parable is the narrative parable, like The Samaritan. I prefer to speak instead of one-liners and extended narratives. What distinguishes the one-liners is not the explicit comparison; all parables have a comparative element. Rather it is their compression. Parable, because of its shortness, is already a compressed form, but one-liners are extremely compressed. Their demands on the hearer are correspondingly intense. While the narrative parables are a form that the rabbis greatly developed, the one-liner is almost completely absent from rabbinic literature.

seed grows into a great tree. This contest between the distinctive voice and common wisdom is a central problem in the interpretation of the parables of Jesus.

Parable as metaphor

A parable is a comparison. The Greek work, *parabole*, indicates this feature — something thrown beside something else. And many of Jesus' parables and rabbinic parables begin with the formula, "it is like . . ." C. H. Dodd accented this aspect of parable in his famous definition.

> At its simplest the parable is a metaphor or simile drawn from nature or common life, arresting the hearer by its vividness or strangeness, and leaving the mind in sufficient doubt about its precise application to tease it into active thought (p. 5).

Many take metaphors as simply ornaments. In the phrase "sea of troubles" SEA is a metaphor for TROUBLES. The implied comparison is between the expanse of the sea and the amount of troubles one has, perhaps also between sea as stormy and troubles as difficult. This metaphor is not necessary to understand troubles. It says the same thing as "I got a whole lotta troubles." Ornamental metaphors are dispensable.

There is another type of metaphor that we might call poetical, although it is used by others besides poets. This metaphor provides a unique insight into its object. It is more than an ornament; it actually shapes the referent itself. Indeed the particular referent is not available without this metaphor, although other metaphors may also be used for the referent. Shakespeare's "All the world's a stage" is such a poetic metaphor.

> All the world's a stage,
> And all the men and women merely players.
> They have their exits and their entrances,
> And one man in his time plays many parts.
> *As You Like It*, 2.7.139–142

Shakespeare's metaphor is actually rather complex. Stage is synecdoche, in which the part, the stage, stands for the whole, the play. The essential metaphor here is "life is a play." And the playwright works out the elements of a play to depict life. The world is the stage, we play roles, roles that vary at different stages of our lives. Although so much quoted that it now sounds trite, Shakespeare's line is not mere ornament. We actually do view and experience life as a play. We play out various roles, view ourselves as having different personas in different situations, and much of therapy is learning a new script to change our lives. Shakespeare's metaphor is profound in its relation to its referent because it gives that referent shape and meaning. Without the metaphor, life becomes shapeless.

Frequently, poetic metaphors that seek to dislodge a myth must take an offensive stance towards the referent. There has to be some shock and inappropriateness to the metaphor. Emily Dickinson frequently uses metaphors in this way.

> I felt a Funeral, in my Brain,
> And Mourners to and fro
> Kept treading — treading — till it seemed
> That Sense was breaking through —
> P. 340 (Franklin Edition)

It may be that Dickinson is here describing depression, although the referent is suppressed. But thinking of mental activity as a funeral is a shock. The rhythm of the mourners' treading to and fro creates in visual and auditory images the experience of the steady beat of feet on the floor, until the last line in which the mourners' treading becomes sense breaking through. Such an image of a funeral does not naturally lead to an expectation of heightened sensation but of despair. Yet the image works, and it offers a new and different way to think about experience.

Jesus' parables often employ poetic metaphors that shock and give offense, although the tradition has tried to hide or overcome that offense. Comparing the kingdom of God to leaven or a mustard seed are two such metaphors. They are shocking and in the case of the leaven offensive, since the expected metaphor in Israel is unleavened, the ancient metaphor of the holy. Many of the characters in the narrative parables likewise seem scandalous as metaphors for the kingdom. The master in the Shrewd Manager expects exorbitant profits and the manager cheats him out of them.

Such strong metaphors are clearly intended to expose and attack the conventional myths, the common wisdom. But they are not just attacks. For those who can use these new metaphors to re-imagine their lives, a new world is born — they live in a different reality from the conventional world created by myth.

In the following passage, one of the great modern parable tellers captures the essence of the parable as a contest between the unnamable and the everyday.

> Many complain that the words of the wise are always merely parables and of no use in daily life, which is the only life we have. When the sage says: "Go over," he does not mean that we should cross to some actual place, which we could do anyhow if the labor were worth it; he means some fabulous yonder, something unknown to us, something too that he cannot designate more precisely, and therefore cannot help us here in the very least. All these parables really set out to say merely that the incomprehensible is incomprehensible, and we know that already. But the cares we have to struggle with every day: that is a different matter.
>
> Concerning this a man once said: Why such reluctance? If you only followed the parables you yourselves would become parables and with that rid of all your daily cares.
>
> Another said: I bet that is also a parable.
>
> The first said: You have won.
>
> The second said: But unfortunately only in parable.
>
> The first said: No, in reality: in parable you have lost.
>
> FRANZ KAFKA, *Parables and Paradoxes*, P. 11

Kafka reminds us that to understand the parables of Jesus we are engaged in a contest to recover that language from the everydayness of myth and common wisdom. Or as Jesus said, "Those who have ears, let them hear."

3

Leaven

The Leaven

Heaven's imperial rule is like leaven that a woman took
    and concealed in three measures of flour
    until it was all leavened
        MATT 13:33

What does God's imperial rule remind me of?
It is like leaven that a woman took
    and concealed in three measures of flour
    until it was all leavened.
        LUKE 13:20–21 (Scholars Version modified)

The Father's imperial rule is like [a] woman.
She took a little leaven, [hid] it in dough,
and made it into large loaves of bread.
        THOMAS 96

The parable of the Leaven received the highest number of red votes of any parable among the participants of the Jesus Seminar. This occurred for several reasons. The parable occurs both in Q, The Synoptic Sayings Source, and the Gospel of Thomas. This means that it is independently attested in two very early Christian documents. Even more important, many members of the Seminar took the parable's provocative character as typical of Jesus.

The parable occurs at Matt 13:33 and Luke 13:20–21. Both gospels pair it with the Mustard Seed. The wording of the parable itself is nearly identical in Matthew and Luke, although the latter introduces it with a question. The nearly verbatim agreement indicates that this was the wording in Q.

The Gospel of Thomas version of the parable is somewhat different because it reverses the order of the leaven and woman, making her the subject of the sentence. Also, the three measures disappears

The Synoptic Puzzle and Q

The similarities between and among the three synoptic gospels, Matthew, Mark, and Luke, are striking. The three are called "synoptic" because they present a "common view" of Jesus. Most scholars believe that Matthew and Luke employed Mark as the basis of their gospels, to which they added other materials, especially from a hypothetical document Q. There are powerful arguments to support this conclusion:

1. Agreement between Matthew and Luke begins where Mark begins and ends where Mark ends.

2. Matthew reproduces about 90% of Mark, Luke about 50%. They often reproduce Mark in the same order. When they disagree, either Matthew or Luke supports the sequence in Mark.

3. In segments the three have in common, verbal agreement averages about 50%.

4. In the triple tradition — segments all three have in common — Matthew and Mark often agree against Luke, and Luke and Mark often agree against Matthew, but Matthew and Luke rarely agree against Mark.

These facts and the close examination of agreements and disagreements in minute detail have led scholars to conclude that Mark is the adopted basis of Matthew and Luke.

This conclusion leads to further observations:

5. Mark is responsible for the chronological outline of the life of Jesus represented by the synoptics; Matthew and Luke do not have independent evidence for the order of events.

7. Mark is the earliest of the three.

8. The material common to Matthew and Luke but absent from Mark is designated as Q, which is an abbreviation of the German word *Quelle*, meaning "source."

Q is a hypothetical construct. No independent copy of it exists. But it is widely believed that the passages in Matthew and Luke that are almost the same, and that did not come from Mark, must have come from this lost source, Q. The non-Markan passages common to Matthew and Luke agree word-for-word so often that Q must have

and instead the outcome is "large loaves of bread." Thus Thomas initiates the interpretive move that sees this parable as an example of increasing from small beginning to large outcome. Thomas turns it into a parable of growth.

The parable of Leaven has also given translators difficulty because

been a written document and not simply a body of material that Matthew and Luke took from oral tradition. The theory that Q and Mark were literary sources for the Gospels of Matthew and Luke is called the Two Source Theory; this theory was first proposed about 150 years ago.

Q is a collection of the sayings of Jesus, similar in form to the Gospel of Thomas. Unlike the sayings in Thomas, however, most of the sayings in Q are gathered into discourses. One of these is the Sermon on the Mount (Matthew) or Plain (Luke).

The Two Source Theory

The Two Source Theory is the view that Matthew and Luke made use of two written sources — Mark and the Sayings Gospels Q — in composing their gospels.

of its compression and use of terms unfamiliar to a modern reader. Translators are always trying to find contemporary terms or words that will make it easier for a modern reader to understand ancient texts. They want to make their translation transparent. A quick look at the various translations given below indicates some of the problems with this parable.

Translations

The King James translation can represent a traditional translation. "It is like leaven which a woman took and hid in three measures of meal till the whole was leavened." The KJ uses words like leaven and three measures, which are difficult for moderns to understand.

Most translations do not know what to do with the woman hiding the leaven in the dough. The Greek does not seem to make much sense to them, so they have the woman either mixing or kneading the dough.

Most of the translations stick with three measures even though it is a measuring unit we no longer use today. Three measures is a very large amount, which is where Thomas probably gets the idea of large loaves. The NIV gives up trying to translate three measures and simply says "a large amount of flour," reminiscent of the Gospel of Thomas. Today's English Version tries to give an equivalent amount, a bushel of flour. In a similar vein the Scholars Version translates the phrase as fifty pounds. While it is true that three measures has little significance for a modern reader, for an ancient reader it would have a great resonance.

Compression

This short review of the problems of translation provides us with a roadmap to understand this parable. Many of the problems of translation result from the parable's highly compressed language. It is a compression that we miss. Our first task is to decompress the parable so that we may begin to understand how its original audience would have heard it.

Leaven

In his definition of parable, C.H. Dodd accented their everydayness as well as their vividness or strangeness. The Leaven is a fine

King James

It is like	which a	and hid	in three	till the whole
leaven	woman took		measures	was leavened.
			of meal	

New Revised Standard Edition

It is like	that a	and mixed in	with three	until all
yeast	woman took		measures	of it was
			of flour	leavened.

Revised English Bible

It is like	which a	and mixed	with three	till it was all
yeast	woman took		measures	leavened.
			of flour	

New American Bible

It is like	which a	to knead into	three	until the
yeast	woman took		measures	whole mass of
			of flour	dough began
				to rise.

New International Version

It is like	that a	and mixed	into a large	until it worked
yeast	woman took		amount	all through the
			of flour	dough.

Today's English Version

A woman	some yeast	and mixes it	a bushel	until the
takes		with	of flour	whole batch
				of dough rises.

Scholar's Version

| It is like | that a | and concealed | in fifty pounds | until it was all |
| leaven | woman took | | of flour | leavened. |

example of both everydayness and everydayness gone astray. The very fact that the woman is making the bread herself indicates a rural, peasant background. In urban areas you bought bread at a bakery. At both Ostia Antica and Pompeii there are remains of large bakeries. Here the scene is different. We are in a rural village, watching a peasant woman preparing to bake bread.

In the ancient world the process of leavening frequently stood as a metaphor for moral corruption. The very distinctiveness of leaven supported this metaphor. Just as a decomposing corpse swells up, so does a leavened loaf. A modern example is the swollen corpse of road kill. That corpse swells up for the same reason that bread swells up — fermentation.

The New Testament contains several examples of this negative use of leaven. In Mark's Gospel Jesus warns the disciples concerning the leaven of the Pharisees and the leaven of Herod (Mark 8:15). This occurs in a situation where the Pharisees have just challenged Jesus to give them a sign (i.e., to perform a miracle), which he refuses to do. In Mark the leaven of the Pharisees would seem to be a simple request for a sign that corrupts the whole enterprise. Matthew interprets the "leaven of the Pharisees" to be their teaching (Matt 16:12), while for Luke it is their hypocrisy (Luke 12:1).

Twice Paul quotes the proverb, "A little leaven leavens the whole lump." In Gal 5:9 Paul uses the proverb to warn against a person who is leading the Galatians astray by demanding that they be circumcised. In 1 Cor 5:6–8 Paul weaves the proverb into a larger analogy. One can almost hear Paul's chain of associations, from leaven to unleavened, to the paschal lamb on the feast of unleavened bread, to Jesus' sacrifice as the paschal lamb, back to leaven (malice) and unleavened (sincerity and truth).

> [6] Your boasting is not a good thing. Do you not know that a little leaven leavens the whole batch of dough? [7] Clean out the old leaven so that you may be a new batch, as you really are unleavened. For our paschal lamb, Christ, has been sacrificed. [8] Therefore, let us celebrate the festival, not with the old leaven, the leaven of malice and evil, but with the unleavened bread of sincerity and truth.
>
> 1 COR 5:6–8 (my translation)

The use of the proverb in Paul reminds us of the American proverb, "one rotten apple spoils the whole barrel." Similarly, leaven functions as a metaphor for the corruption of the whole batch of dough. Likewise Paul's mixing of the proverb with the analogy of the Paschal lamb recalls for us the opposite of leaven, namely unleavened.

In the Hebrew Bible unleavened bread is a powerful symbol of the holy. During the feast of Passover, the feast of unleavened bread, all leavened bread was to be cleansed out of the house.

When we reflect how leaven is a product of rotten bread and is associated with a corpse, we began to see how it can serve as a power-

Feast of Unleavened Bread

[15] Seven days you shall eat unleavened bread; on the first day you shall remove leaven from your houses, for whoever eats leavened bread from the first day until the seventh day shall be cut off from Israel. [16] On the first day you shall hold a solemn assembly, and on the seventh day a solemn assembly; no work shall be done on those days; only what everyone must eat, that alone may be prepared by you. [17] You shall observe the festival of unleavened bread, for on this very day I brought your companies out of the land of Egypt: you shall observe this day throughout your generations as a perpetual ordinance.

EXODUS 12:15–17

ful metaphor for corruption and how its opposite, unleavened bread, can serve as a metaphor for the sacred and holy.

The very beginning of the parable with the simple word "leaven," would throw an audience off guard and maybe into a panic. For leaven is surely no correct symbol of the kingdom of God.

The Woman hid

The role of women in the ancient world is very complex and debated. We need to avoid oversimplifications. In general the situation of women in the Roman Empire was not favorable. The Roman Empire was hierarchically structured with males in all the dominant positions. The emperor was male, the Senate was male, and the governors were male. It was a patriarchical society.

In all ancient society, the family replicated this hierarchical structure. Women were subject to their husbands or fathers. While it is not true to say that in general women were viewed as unclean and men clean, it is true that in religion, especially in purity codes, women were at a disadvantage.

In the normal process of baking one might expect a woman to be kneading the dough. There is nothing untoward about her role here. But as a parable for the kingdom of God, a woman's role as an emblem of the sacred becomes highly problematic.

Again, there is nothing wrong with the kingdom of God being hidden. But in this parable an unexpected word is used for hiding.

"Concealed" — *krypto* (Luke) or *enkrypto* (Matthew) — is a much more negative term for hiding than the more neutral *kalypto*. *Krypto* has a sense of concealment. It is the root of the English word encrypt, meaning to keep secret by means of a code.

The parable pictures a woman concealing the leaven in the lump of dough.

Three measures

A number of translations have tried to make the modern reader aware of how much flour the woman is kneading. The enormous amount of about fifty pounds is enough to feed over a hundred people. But three measures is more than just a large amount.

In Israel's tradition, three measures has a resonance in the tradition that conjures up a much larger tale. Oral performers frequently "quote" by means of metonymy; they name a part to indicate the whole, just as we click on an icon to view a whole new web page. They do not quote word for word or verbatim, as do literate folks who cite a text. In an oral world references rely on memory and are commonly allusive, not direct. The performer draws from a repertoire or thesaurus of a shared cultural stock of stories and tales, myths and legends.

Three measures refers to a famous story in Genesis 18 concerning the prophecy of the birth of Isaac. In this story three angels, one of whom is Yahweh, visit Abraham and among the items Sarah prepares for them are cakes made from three measures of flour.

When the parable employs the term three measures it conjures up from the audience's repertoire the story of Abraham and the birth of Isaac. In parable it suggests a comparison between the woman's actions and the birth of Isaac. Now we begin to understand the difference between parabolic or oral thinking and our own literate, more abstract way of thinking. In parable "three measures" serves to compare the event of Isaac's birth with the event of the parable. Literally and abstractly it makes little sense. But parable is a concrete way of thinking, not an abstract way.

Until it's all leavened

The leavening process keeps working until everything is leavened, until the whole batch of dough is leavened through and through, until everything is corrupted. Hosea 7:4 presents an interesting parallel

Abraham's Visitors

¹The LORD appeared to Abraham by the oaks of Mamre, as he sat at the entrance of his tent in the heat of the day. ² He looked up and saw three men standing near him. When he saw them, he ran from the tent entrance to meet them, and bowed down to the ground. ³ He said, "My lord, if I find favor with you, do not pass by your servant. ⁴ Let a little water be brought, and wash your feet, and rest yourselves under the tree. ⁵ Let me bring a little bread, that you may refresh yourselves, and after that you may pass on — since you have come to your servant." So they said, "Do as you have said." ⁶ And Abraham hastened into the tent to Sarah, and said, "Make ready quickly three measures of choice flour, knead it, and make cakes." ⁷Abraham ran to the herd, and took a calf, tender and good, and gave it to the servant, who hastened to prepare it. ⁸ Then he took curds and milk and the calf that he had prepared, and set it before them; and he stood by them under the tree while they ate.

GENESIS 18:1–8

with this passage showing how the metaphor of leavening points to its inevitable course, its total corrupting activity.

> They are all adulterers;
> they are like a heated oven,
> whose baker does not need to stir the fire,
> from the kneading of the dough until it is leavened.
> HOSEA 7:4

Kneading the parable

For Matthew, Luke, and Thomas the parable of the Leaven is a metaphor for the kingdom of God, as most translations have the phrase. The difference in phrasing between kingdom of *God* and kingdom of *Heaven* represents a difference between Jewish usage and gentile. Out of reverence, Jews normally avoid mentioning the name of God. Thus in manuscripts of the Hebrew Bible the four letters of God's name (the tetragrammaton) are left unpronounced or are vocalized with the vowels of the word Adonai. To this day, in printed editions of the Hebrew Bible, the tetragrammaton is printed with the vowel markings of Adonai. This is how the English word Jehovah was created. The consonants are from the tetragrammaton and the vowels from Adonai. Matthew's kingdom of Heaven is the standard Jewish usage, while Luke's kingdom of God represents gentile usage. Thomas's "the Father's imperial rule" is that gospel's normal usage, and Matthew on occasion uses a similar phrase. All of which is to say that the apparent differences make no difference.

Matthew	Luke	Thomas
The kingdom of Heaven is like . . .	To what shall I compare the kingdom of God?	The kingdom of the Father is like . . .
Heaven's imperial rule like. . . .	What does God's imperial rule remind me of?	The Father's imperial rule is like . . .

But how to translate the Greek represented by these English translations is another problem. The Greek word is *basileia*. From the root of this word comes the English word basilica, which was the Roman word for a very large public building, the emperor's administrative offices, where he conducted his business. The *basil* root is extended to *basileus* for the male ruler and *basileuo* for the activity of ruling. When we translate this phrase as "kingdom of God" it conjures up a religious term for most, and for some it means heaven or life after death.

We live in a democracy and so the term "kingdom" sounds quite old fashioned and other worldly. In the ancient world, *basileia* has to do with royal administration. Specifically *the baseleia* in the first century was the Roman Empire. This royal rule was not benevolent. *Pax Romana* was Augustus' great gift to the people following his defeat of Mark Anthony and Cleopatra at Actium in 31 BCE, and the fruit of his long reign. But it was *pax* only if you were *Romana*, otherwise it was *oppressio*, oppression. Augustus was the emperor who brought order to the Empire, but in the process destroyed the Republic and introduced increasingly harsh and autocratic rule. Augustus' own account of his reign, written at the end of his life and commemorating his seventy–fifth birthday (13 CE), was set up in all in the major cities of the Empire and shows the importance of power and war in Roman peace.

This excursus on history has a vital point. Jesus' audience would inevitably hear the *basileia* of God as opposing the *basileia* of Caesar. Therefore I suggest that we translate *basileia* as empire, and so the phrase would be "the empire of God." Some will object that empire is too negative when applied to God, especially in the aftermath of Star Wars, and Ronald Reagan's famous remark about the evil empire. But this negative connotation is precisely the point. From the point of view of those oppressed by the Roman Empire, *basileia* has a negative connotation. Translating the phrase as "empire of God" reminds us implicitly of its opposite. The fact that Jesus employs the term empire, the noun for the ruling activity, and not the noun for the ruler, emperor or king, perhaps reinforces this. His usage is strange since the reference to God as King or Emperor is common in the Hebrew Bible and its Greek translation, the Septuagint, while empire of God is absent.

Translations represent conventions. Jesus and his contemporaries did not use "kingdom" or "empire" because they obviously did not speak English. What we are searching for is an English word that will have the proper connotation and range of reference. Kingdom seems to me too abstract and otherworldly because it invokes a fairy tale world. Empire has the sense of domination, power, and threat that *basileia* demands.

Just what does empire of God mean?

What does the parable tell us about the empire of God? Or should we ask, what the empire of God tells us about the parable? These are important questions. What tells us about what? Does the parable tell us about the empire or it is the other way around? For a long time, we have resisted the implications of the parable of the Leaven because it was assumed that the empire of God, or anything associated with God, could not have such negative associations. But my contention is that Jesus told parables to let people in on his experience of God. Parables were his way of making God available to them. Actually, empire of God is a symbol used to make God available to folks, to provide them an alternative to their everyday life in the empire of Caesar or in the kingdom of Caesar's puppet, Herod Antipas.

If we listen to the parable it says something like this.

"The empire of God is like moral corruption."

Well of course, that is a very bad start. Most folks in Jesus' audience would have blanched at the first term "leaven," for the empire of God cannot be like leaven, but should be unleavened. Perhaps they would snicker that the empire of Caesar is more like leaven.

"which a woman took."

Again how can a woman, weak as she is, have anything to do with

Res Gestae Divi Augustus
Things accomplished by the Divine One

. . . I returned to Rome from Spain and Gaul after settling the affairs of those provinces with success. The Senate, to commemorate my return, ordered an altar to Pax Augusta to be consecrated in the Campus Martius, at which it decreed that the magistrates, priests, and Vestal Virgins should celebrate an anniversary sacrifice.

Whereas our ancestors have willed that the gateway of Janus Quirinus should be shut, whenever victorious peace is secured by sea and by land throughout the empire of the Roman people, and whereas before my birth twice only in all is it on record that the gateway has been shut, three times under my principate has the Senate decreed that it should be shut . . .

I conquered the pirates and gave peace to the seas. In that war I handed over to their masters for punishment nearly 30,000 slaves who had run away from their owners, and taken up arms against the republic.

The whole of Italy of its own free will took the oath of fidelity to me, and demanded me as its leader in the war of which Actium was the crowning victory. . . .

I extended the frontiers of all the provinces of the Roman people, which had as neighbors races not obedient to our empire.

I restored peace to all the provinces of Gaul and Spain and to Germany . . .

Peace too I caused to be established in the Alps from the region nearest to the Hadriatic as far as the Tuscan sea . . .

My fleet sailed along the Ocean from the mouth of the Rhine as far towards the east as the borders of the Cimbri, whither no Roman before that time had penetrated either by land or sea. The Cimbri and the Charydes and the Semnones and other German peoples of the same region through their envoys petitioned for my friendship and that of the Roman people.

By my command and under my auspices two armies were led almost at the same time, one into Ethiopia, the other into that part of Arabia

God's empire? But if it is like leaven, then there is a certain logic, a weird logic, to the parable.

"and concealed . . ."

Does she do it while no one is looking? How can she keep it concealed? Will folks be unaware that it is leavened bread? After all most bread in the ancient world was flat bread, like tortillas or pita.

"in three measures of flour . . ."

which is called Felix; and large forces of the enemy belonging to both races were killed in battle, and many towns captured. . .

Egypt I added to the empire of the Roman people.

Greater Armenia, on the murder of its king Artaxes, I could have made into a province, but I preferred, following the precedent of our ancestors, and acting through Tiberius Nero, who was then my step-son, to hand it over as a kingdom to Tigranes, son of Artavasdes, and grandson of king Tigranes. Afterwards, when the same race revolted and rebelled, I subdued it by means of my son, Gaius, and handed it over to the rule of king Ariobarzanes, the son of Artabazus, king of the Medes; and after his death, to his son, Artavasdes. On the latter being killed, I sent out to the kingdom Tigranes, a scion of the royal family of Armenia. . . .

In my sixth and seventh consulships, after I had extinguished the civil wars, having been put in supreme possession of the whole empire by the universal consent of all, I transferred the republic from my own power into the free control of the Senate and Roman people.

For which service I received the appellation of Augustus by decree of the Senate, and the door-posts of my house were publicly decked with laurel leaves; the civic crown was fixed up above my gate, and a golden shield set up in the Julian senate-house, which, as its inscription testifies, was granted to me by the Senate and Roman people to commemorate my virtue, clemency, justice, and piety.

After that time I stood before all others in dignity, but of actual power I possessed no more than my colleagues in each several magistracy.

While I was holding my thirteenth consulship, the Senate and equestrian order and the whole Roman people gave me the title of father of my country, and decreed that the title should be inscribed in the vestibule of my house and in the senate-house and in the forum of Augustus, under the chariot which was set up in my honor by decree of the Senate.

At the time when I wrote these records, I was in my seventy-sixth year.

BARRETT, *New Testament Background*, P. 2–4.

Now we are getting somewhere. Finally an image of great size, an image appropriate to God. And this tells us we are on the right track. Three measures assures us that this is after all the empire of God. What a huge banquet she is preparing, enough for a hundred people! This is an event like the birth of Isaac. Is she preparing the messianic banquet?

"until it was all leavened . . ."

Until it has worked its way through everything, until it has corrupted the whole mass of dough. Surely such total corruption is nonsense as a way of talking about God or experiencing God. What is this about?

Perhaps we should ask ourselves for whom would this parable be good news and, by implication, for whom would it be bad news? Several answers are evident. This parable would be good news for women. It gives them a major role in the empire of God, just the way they are, doing their normal everyday activities, baking bread, even leavened bread.

For all those who are leaven in their society, this parable assures them that the empire of God is like them. In Jesus' society this was a large majority of people. All those who were unable for one reason or another to observe the purity code would be leaven and that would be most folks. "Congratulations to you poor" is not an appeal to the bottom 10% as it would be in America, but to at least 80% of the population of first century Palestine who lived a subsistence existence. Times were hard in Galilee.

Of course, for all those who were doing well under the current régime, this parable would be bad news. God was not like what they imagined or the scriptures had predicted. God was not like unleavened bread, but leavened. The boundary of the sacred established by the Feast of Unleavened Bread is eliminated.

Sometimes it helps to translate a parable into contemporary terms as long as we are aware of what might be lost. A female student of mine once proposed the following modern equivalent. "God's overwhelming love is like cancer that invaded a woman's breast until it had consumed all of her, even in her Sunday finery." It is just as difficult to conceive of God's love as breast cancer as it is the empire of God as leaven. The student was dying of breast cancer and remarked that her form of the parable had finally allowed her to see that God was on her side even in her battle with cancer.

The parable of the Leaven reminds us that naming the situation, truly describing it, often produces more hope than the false expectation that by some magic wand it can all be set aright.

4

Mustard Seed

The Mustard Seed

> It is like a mustard seed that a man took
> and tossed into his garden.
> It grew
> and became a tree
> and the birds of the sky roosted in its branches.
> LUKE 13:18-19

The Mustard Seed is often paralleled with the Leaven, as though they make the same point. Early in the tradition Q, and then Matthew and Luke who draw upon Q, first grouped the two parables together. Similarly, since the mustard seed is proverbially small, Mark and Thomas make much of the contrast between small beginnings and large outcomes.

Yet when we begin to examine the parable in its various versions more closely, things begin to grow out of control.

Q/Luke 13:18–19	Thomas 20	Mark 4:30–32	Matt 13:31–2
1. [18] He said there-fore, "What is the kingdom of God like? And to what should I compare it?	The disciples said to Jesus, "Tell us what Heaven's imperial rule is like?", He said to them,	"With what can we compare the kingdom of God, or what parable will we use for it?	[31] He put before them another parable: The kingdom of heaven is

35

Q/Luke 13:18–19	Thomas 20	Mark 4:30–32	Matt 13:31–2
2. [19] It is like a mustard seed	"It is like a mustard seed.	[31] It is like a mustard seed,	like a mustard seed
3. that someone took and sowed in the garden;	<It's> the smallest of all seeds, but when it falls on prepared soil,	which, when sown upon the ground, is the smallest of all the seeds on earth; [32] yet when it is sown	that someone took and sowed in his field; [32] it is the smallest of all the seeds,
4. it grew and became a tree,	it produces a large branch	it grows up and becomes the greatest of all shrubs, and puts forth large branches,	but when it has grown it is the greatest of shrubs and becomes a tree,
5. and the birds of the air made nests in its branches."	and becomes a shelter for birds of the sky.	so that the birds of the air can make nests in its shade."	so that the birds of the air come and make nests in its branches."

I have arranged the texts from the simplest to the most overgrown, on the theory that traditions tend to become more complex as they develop, not simpler. I take Luke to be the Q text. Matthew conflates Q and Mark. It's the smallest of all seeds, but it becomes the greatest of shrubs and then turns into a tree: a real biological miracle. Mark seems to have introduced the note about smallest to greatest into his parable. It is a well known editorial technique of Mark that when he inserts a phrase into a larger unit, he frequently repeats the preceding term after the insertion, so there is a repetition of "when it is sown." You can see this technique clearly at work in Mark's story of the cure of the paralytic (Mark 2:1–12). Into that story the author inserts a debate between Jesus and the Pharisees on the forgiveness of sins (verses 6–10a). When the story returns to the paralytic, the phrase "he says to the paralytic" is repeated (verses 5 and 10).

That leaves Q and Thomas. The Jesus Seminar preferred the Thomas version, primarily because in Thomas the mustard seed does not produce a tree, but a large branch. This is what happens in nature. But I disagree with their decision. The note about the smallest of seeds is proverbial and could easily be an addition. Furthermore, Thomas did the same thing with leaven, making the move from small leaven to large loaves. In the parable of the Lost Sheep, in Thomas the shepherd goes after the largest sheep (Thomas 107). Likewise in the parable of the Fishnet, the fisherman keeps a fine large fish (Thomas 8). This note about large would seem to be part of Thomas' editing, not original. As Sherlock Holmes observed, "When you have eliminated the impossible, whatever remains, however improbable, must be the truth" (*The Sign of the Four*). Therefore, I take the Q (Luke) version to be the earliest extant form.

What then are we to make of a mustard plant that grows into a tree? A biological misfit? Sometimes the Greek word for tree is used for a large plant, but I don't think that explanation is necessary. Rather I suggest we look to the artistry of the parable teller.

Although not as strange or provocative as leaven, the mustard seed is a strange analogy for the empire of God. The mustard plant is an annual and it grows wild. Pliny well summarizes the situation.

Pliny on Mustard

It [mustard] grows entirely wild, though it is improved by being transplanted: but on the other hand when it has once been sown it is scarcely possible to get the place free of it, as the seed when it falls germinates at once.*
Natural History, 29.54.170 (LOEB)

While the plant has many good uses, it is a weed.

Pliny's warning becomes even more relevant when we notice where the man plants the seed, in his garden. Just on a common sense level he is asking for trouble. But more than common sense is at stake. Fundamental to the purity code of Leviticus and its later elaboration in *Mishnah* is that things that are not alike are not to be mixed.

Leviticus 19:19 provides the fundamental citation on which all the kosher provisions are based. The reference to *Mishnah* Kilayim shows that planting mustard seed in a garden is clearly prohibited.

---

*Pliny the Elder, (AD 23–79) was the author of thirty-seven books of *Natural History*, a type of encyclopedia that attempted to summarize everything known about nature. "Nature, which is to say life, is my subject." He was commander of the Roman Fleet at Misenum and was killed investigating the eruption of Mount Vesuvius in 79 AD.

Leviticus 19:19

You shall not let your animals breed with a different kind; you shall not sow your field with two kinds of seed; nor shall you put on a garment made of two different materials.

Mishnah Kilayim 3.2

Not every kind of seed may be sown in a garden, but any kind of vegetable may be sown therein. Mustard and small beans arc deemed a kind of seed and large beans a kind of vegetable.
DANBY

But instead of the mustard plants taking over the garden, the parable veers in another direction. If we construe this parable with literal mindedness, the mustard plant growing into a tree makes no sense. But if we hear it as an oral performance with ears attuned to image and poetry, then the end of the parable makes a certain kind of sense. We should not allow the supposed everydayness of the parables to reduce them to the trite or the overly literal. In the Leaven, the woman is baking an outlandish amount of bread. Or to take a contemporary example, in the Beatles song, Eleanor Rigby keeps her face in a jar. It is a very striking image, but hardly to be taken literally.

As we have noted before, in oral story telling one does not normally quote literally because these are not literal, text minded folks. Rather they quote by allowing a part to stand for the whole. The part conjures up a larger image from the common story–telling tradition. The clues here are "tree" and "the birds of the air made nests in its branches." These two references conjure up the mighty cedar of Lebanon. Two texts from Ezekiel and one from Daniel clearly belong to the same narrative tradition. Each refers to a mighty tree with birds nesting in its branches or shade.

Ezekiel 17:22–23
(about restored Israel)

²² Thus says the Lord GOD:
I myself will take a sprig from the lofty top of a cedar;
I will set it out.
I will break off a tender one from the topmost of its young twigs;

Ezekiel 31:2–6
(about Egypt & Assyria)

² Mortal, say to Pharaoh king of Egypt and to his hordes: Whom are you like in your greatness?
³Consider Assyria, a cedar of Lebanon, with fair branches and forest shade, and of great height, its top among the

Daniel 4:10–12
(about Babylonia)

¹⁰ Upon my bed this is what I saw;
there was a tree at the center of the earth,
and its height was great.
¹¹ The tree grew great and strong,
its top reached to heaven,

I myself will plant it
on a high and lofty
mountain.
23 On the mountain
height of Israel
I will plant it,
in order that it may pro-
duce boughs and bear
fruit,
and become a noble
cedar.
Under it every kind of
bird will live;
in the shade of its
branches will nest
winged creatures of
every kind.

clouds. 4 The waters
nourished it, the deep
made it grow tall, mak-
ing its rivers flow
around the place it was
planted, sending forth
its streams to all the
trees of the field. 5 So it
towered high above all
the trees of the field; its
boughs grew large and
its branches long, from
abundant water in its
shoots. 6 *All the birds of*
the air made their nests
in its boughs; under its
branches all the animals
of the field gave birth to
their young; and *in its*
shade all great nations
lived.

and it was visible to the
ends of the whole earth.
12 Its foliage was beautiful,
its fruit abundant,
and it provided food for
all.
The animals of the field
found shade under it,
the birds of the air
nested in its branches,
and from it all living
beings were fed.

This implicit "quoting" of the cedar of Lebanon juxtaposes in the parable the image of the weed-like mustard plant with that of the mighty cedar. It doesn't turn the mustard bush into a "real" tree, much less a mighty cedar, but it draws a contrast in expectations. It raises the question, What should an empire be like: a mustard plant or the noble, mighty cedar?

The answer is clear. An empire is more like a cedar of Lebanon. But Jesus' parable burlesques this assumption. It pokes fun at our expectation that an empire must be a mighty anything. Caesar's empire or Herod's client kingdom might have such pretensions. But for Jesus, God's empire is more pervasive than dominant. It is like a pungent weed that takes over everything and in which the birds of the air can nest; it bears little if any resemblance to the mighty, majestic, and noble symbol of empire of Israel or Caesar. Take your choice, says the parable.

The history of this parable's interpretation is a clear example of how Jesus' own language betrayed him, because the tradition had a clear preference for the cedar of Lebanon. Thomas draws on the small to large metaphor, implicit in the small mustard seed and the giant tree, while Mark goes him one better and goes from "smallest" to "greatest," and so the burlesque implicit in the contrast is lost.

The multiple versions of this parable can serve as a paradigm of the fate of Jesus' parables. Frequently the very metaphorical structure to which he is drawing a contrast subverts his own parable and turns it against itself. The Leaven escaped that fate in Q and fell victim to it in Thomas. Q's coupling of the Mustard Plant with Leaven led Matthew to interpret the Leaven by means of the Mustard Plant. In Matthew the mustard plant is not only the smallest of seeds, but it grows into the greatest of shrubs and then a tree. Thus the smallest to greatest image dominates Matthew's parable (although absent in his Q source).

Why did the parable of the Leaven and the Mustard Plant fail in the later tradition? Why did Christian preaching so perversely misunderstand them? The fault lies in the language of the parable. In these two parables Jesus took on the fundamental assumptions of his society — and nearly every human society — about how God acts. How are we to imagine God's activity? As leaven or unleavened? As a mustard plant or a mighty cedar? The tradition either pretended or preferred not to hear in parable his re-imagined God.

5

The Empty Jar

The Empty Jar

The [Father's] Imperial rule is like a woman who was carrying a
[jar] full of meal.
While she was walking along [a] distant road,
        the handle of the jar broke
        and the meal spilled behind her [along] the road.
She didn't know it;
        she hadn't noticed a problem.
When she reached her house,
        she put the jar down
        and discovered that it was empty.
        THOMAS 97

Parables in the Gospel of Thomas

The abundance of parables in Thomas sets it apart from the other apocryphal gospels or even the gospel of John. Of its thirteen parables, moreover, eleven have parallels in the synoptic gospels. Naturally enough, no doubt, these have attracted more interest than the two which are unique to Thomas, but clearly the existence of this group of parables in Thomas points to the primitive character of at least some of the tradition contained in that gospel. The famous parable scholar Joachim Jeremias, a moderate and cautious exegete, treated the parables in the Gospel of Thomas as an independent witness to the parables of Jesus in the sixth German edition of his *Parables of Jesus* (1962).

Even more noteworthy than the number of these parables is their lack of allegorical interpretation. This has led to considerable scholarly debate over the significance of the omission:

- Did Thomas delete the allegories he found in the synoptic sources?
- Did the parable tradition preserved in the Gospel of Thomas take shape before the parables in the synoptic gospels were allegorized?

Those favoring the first position argue that the author of Thomas has simply stripped away the allegorical elements. For two reasons I find this difficult to accept.

- Narrative is a stronger form than exposition.

The narrative context of the synoptic gospels is secondary and yet it remains fixed in the imagination. For example, it is evident that the parable of the Samaritan did not originally belong to the narrative context which Luke constructed for it. Yet it is hard to understand the parable as anything but an answer to the question, "Who is my neighbor?"

- The parables in Thomas do not contain synoptic redactional elements.

When the synoptic gospels are closely examined, one becomes aware of the distinctive style and vocabulary of each of the authors. Yet that distinctive vocabulary is missing from each of the Gospel of Thomas parallels. If the author of Thomas received the parables in their synoptic forms, how did he manage to strip them entirely of that distinctive vocabulary?

Early in this debate, it was noticed that the Leased Vineyard (Thomas 65; Mark 12:1-8) appeared in Thomas without an allegory and in form almost identical to a reconstruction of the parable proposed by C.H. Dodd many years before the discovery of the Gospel of Thomas. This strongly suggested not only the independence of the Thomas parables from the written synoptic gospels but also its derivation from a very early collection of Jesus' parables.

If the parables in Thomas represent an ancient collection, then the two parables which lack synoptic parallels, the Assassin (Thomas 98) and the Empty Jar (Thomas 97), deserve serious consideration as authentic parables of Jesus.

The Assassin
The Father's imperial rule is like a person who wanted to kill someone powerful. While still at home he drew his sword and thrust it into the wall to find out whether his hand would go in. Then he killed the powerful one.
THOMAS 98

Scholars have been slow to accept these two parables as authentic Jesus parables for two reasons.

• The obvious lack of a synoptic parallel.

Although single attestation has not stopped scholars from highly valuing other synoptic parables — for example, the Samaritan, Shrewd Manager, Vineyard Laborers all were voted red by the Jesus Seminar — the preference for the canon exerts a powerful influence.

• The very limited tradition of interpretation of the Gospel of Thomas and the parables contained in it.

The Empty Jar

Since the Gospel of Thomas was not discovered until 1945, scholars lack an extensive interpretive context in which to set the parable. Yet as early as 1962 the British scholar Hugh Montefiore argued that the parable of the Empty Jar was an authentic Jesus parable. He compared it to the parable of Leaven and the Seed and Harvest (Mark 4:26–29). For him, all three parables referred to the imperceptible coming of the kingdom.

The Empty Jar occurs in the Gospel of Thomas as the middle parable in a series of three: the Leaven, the Empty Jar, and the Assassin. These three parables form a triptych displaying a series of contrasts: little and big, full and empty; powerful and weak. As the middle member of the triptych, the parable is a negative example, an example of loss. Since Thomas is concerned with wisdom, the double repetition of her lack of understanding is important. "She didn't know it; she hadn't noticed a problem." This double emphasis makes the point

The Widow of Zarephath

[8] Then the word of the LORD came to him, saying, [9] "Go now to Zarephath, which belongs to Sidon, and live there; for I have commanded a widow there to feed you." [10] So he set out and went to Zarephath. When he came to the gate of the town, a widow was there gathering sticks; he called to her and said, "Bring me a little water in a vessel, so that I may drink." [11] As she was going to bring it, he called to her and said, "Bring me a morsel of bread in your hand." [12] But she said, "As the LORD your God lives, I have nothing baked, only a handful of meal in a jar, and a little oil in a jug; I am now gathering a couple of sticks, so that I may go home and prepare it for myself and my son, that we may eat it, and die." [13] Elijah said to her, "Do not be afraid; go and do as you have said; but first make me a little cake of it and bring it to me, and afterwards make something for yourself and your son. [14] For thus says the LORD the God of Israel: The jar of meal will not be emptied and the jug of oil will not fail until the day that the LORD sends rain on the earth." [15] She went and did as Elijah said, so that she as well as he and her household ate for many days. [16] The jar of meal was not emptied, neither did the jug of oil fail, according to the word of the LORD that he spoke by Elijah.

1 KINGS 17:8–16

for Thomas: indeed, one of the iterations may well result from Thomas' editorial activity.

When we begin to analyze the parable not as a parable of the Gospel of Thomas, but as a parable of Jesus, we must first focus on the structure of the parable itself. What provides the metaphor for understanding the empire of God? For Montefiore, one of the parable's earliest interpreters, it was the imperceptible coming of the kingdom. The problem with this suggestion is that the jar is empty. Montefiore rightly identifies the lack of perception motif that Thomas accents, but if the coming of the empire is the subject of the parable, then the empire which is coming is not only imperceptible, it's also empty. Others have suggested that the journey is the metaphor, but this does not seem to be a prominent aspect of the woman's story, although a gnostic reading of the story might see the woman's journey as the journey of the soul. Her lack of notice, also a Gnostic element, could also serve as a warning against frittering away the empire by focusing too exclusively on the immediate details of the journey, the path directly in front of us. Nevertheless, the compelling image with which the parable ends is that empty jar.

At the most elementary level of discourse the story is about loss. The woman arrives home empty-handed. The empire, then, is identified with loss, with accident, with emptiness. The parable with the greatest structural similarity is the Rich Farmer (Luke 12:16–20) or the version in Thomas, The Rich Investor (Thomas 63). The man has a great harvest and that night he dies. Both parables move from bounty (full jar, great harvest) to loss (empty jar, death). In some way loss must be a fundamental part of the interpretation.

It is also possible that the story of Elijah's miracle for the widow of Zarephath as told in 1 Kings 17:8–16 lies in the background as a contrast story. When a famine came upon the land, Elijah is told to go to Zarephath where "I have commanded a widow to feed you." He finds a widow at the city gate and asks for a piece of bread. She replies, "As the Lord your God lives, I have nothing baked, only a handful of meal in a jar, and a little oil in a jug." She had been gathering sticks in order to bake some cakes for her child and herself. Elijah commanded her to bake, but bring him the first cake. "For thus says the Lord the God of Israel: 'The jar of meal will not be emptied . . . until the day that the Lord sends rain on the earth.'" She does as Elijah commands, and the prophet, she, and her child have meal throughout the famine. "The jar of meal was not emptied . . . according to the word of the Lord that he spoke by Elijah." The parable of

The Coming of God's Imperial Rule

When asked by the Pharisees when God's imperial rule would come, he answered them, "You won't be able to observe the coming of God's imperial rule. People are not going to be able to say, 'Look, here it is!' or 'Over there!' On the contrary, God's imperial rule is right there in your presence."

LUKE 17:20–21

His disciples said to him, "When will the <Father's> imperial rule come?"

"It will not come by watching for it. It will not be said, 'Look, here! Or 'Look, there!' Rather, the Father's imperial rule is spread out upon the earth, and people don't see it."

THOMAS 113

the Empty Jar presents a contrast to the story of the widow with a full jar. There is no prophet to come to her aid, no eschatological miracle to set things aright.

While the Hebrew Bible story of the widow with the full jar furnishes an interesting contrast to the parable of the Empty Jar, such a reference is not needed to understand the parable. The basic narrative is clear. There is no divine intervention; she goes home empty-handed. The empire is identified not with apocalyptic intervention but with the paradox of divine emptiness.

How might we understand this paradox of divine emptiness? Jesus' saying, The Coming of God's Imperial Rule (Thom 113; Luke 17:20–21) offers a parallel. This saying explicitly rejects the ability of people to point to or observe the empire. "On the contrary, God's imperial rule is right there in your presence." Both the Thomas and Lucan recensions of the saying agree on these two basic points — the empire cannot be observed, but it is present. This presence of the empire — not able to be observed but in your presence, spread out upon the earth but not seen — emphasizes the paradox that the empire is present in absence. There is a divine intervention in the empire, but it cannot be observed.

6

Hidden Treasure

Hidden Treasure

Heaven's imperial rule is like treasure hidden in a field:
when someone finds it,
that person covers it up again,
and out of sheer joy goes
and sells every last possession
and buys that field.
MATT 13:44

The parable of the Treasure starts off with an image appropriate to the empire of God, unlike the Leaven and the Mustard Seed which begin with inappropriate images. Had someone challenged Jesus' use of leaven or mustard seed, he probably would have replied with treasure. And the audience would have replied, "Now that's better."

The parable of the Treasure presses the boundaries of interpretation in several interesting ways. As a one-liner, like the Leaven and the Mustard Seed, it is tightly compressed, but at the same time begins to expand into a more narrative form like the Empty Jar. It does not have the elaborate story form of the large narrative parables like the Samaritan or the Prodigals. But it does imply a story, a scenario, that a hearer must imagine.

The Gospel of Thomas also has a treasure parable, but exactly how it is related to the treasure parable in Matthew is unclear. We will turn to the Thomas parable later in our discussion.

Finding treasure

Found treasure is an unexpected boon. It takes place outside the normal everyday course of events. There is a kind of lawlessness associated with treasure in the sense that it is beyond everyday expectation. This explains the popularity even today of bargain hunting, the possibility of getting something for nothing. Likewise the great attraction of the PBS TV program "Antiques Road Show" is the anticipation that some piece of junk in your closet might turn out to be worth a fortune. When the appraisers ask the guests whether they know the value of their antique, almost invariably they answer, "I have no idea." We all love the thrill of a trifling possession suddenly being worth a fortune, or at least much more than we thought.

Burying treasure was not all that unusual in the ancient world, in the days before banking systems became widespread and safe. Before the Federal Deposit Insurance Corporation with its guaranteed safety of deposits, many people trusted their savings to the mattress. The Jewish historian Josephus (37–about 100 CE) reports that many of the inhabitants of Jerusalem buried their wealth during the siege of Jerusalem. The truth of Josephus' remark can be seen in many museums where we find extensive collections of ancient coins, which are still found in hoards even to this day.

Treasure in Jerusalem

Yet was there no small quantity of the riches that had been in that city still found among its ruins, a great deal of which the Romans dug up; but the greatest part was discovered by those who were captives, and so they carried it away; I mean the gold and the silver, and the rest of that most precious furniture which the Jews had, and which the owners had treasured up under ground, against the uncertain fortunes of war.

JOSEPHUS, *Jewish War*, 7.5.2

The Book of Proverbs also uses the metaphor of searching for and finding treasure to explain how one searches for knowledge of God. Knowledge about God's commands is like finding treasure. In the poem from Proverbs 2 the image is woven into the fabric of the verse and serves to illustrate a feature common to almost all treasure stories: finding comes at the end of the story, and as a reward for good deeds or hard work.

God's Treasure

> ¹My child, if you accept my words
> and treasure up my commandments within you,
> ² making your ear attentive to wisdom
> and inclining your heart to understanding;
> ³ if you indeed cry out for insight,
> and raise your voice for understanding;
> ⁴ if you seek it like silver,
> and search for it as for hidden treasures —
> ⁵ then you will understand the fear of the LORD
> and find the knowledge of God.
>> PROVERBS 2:1–5

Hidden in a field

The Parable of the Treasure in Matthew begins with finding. This observation determines the understanding and appreciation of the parable and sets this story apart from the common run of treasure stories.

The story of Abba Judah can serve as a paradigm. Abba Judah was a holy man who was married to a woman even more righteous than himself. He was famous for caring for the rabbis out of his wealth. But when his circumstances were reduced, he was in despair over what to do. His wife advised him to sell half of his one remaining field and give the proceeds to the rabbis. This part of the story is reminiscent of the Jesus story about the widow giving her last penny to the temple treasury (Mark 12:42–44).

Then, while he was plowing the remaining half of the field, his cow fell and broke its leg. The bad luck of this holy man seems to know no end. Were it not for bad luck, he would have no luck at all.

Finally he is rewarded for his righteousness. God "opened his eyes, and he found a jewel." In the story the finding of the treasure is clearly the work of God rewarding Abba Judah for his righteousness, his generosity even in poverty.

The last part of the story is an acknowledgment, a celebration and acclamation of the worthiness of Abba Judah to receive this great reward of treasure. At the end he sits down with the rabbis, fulfilling

Tevye's wish in *Fiddler on the Roof*. He would sit in the synagogue all day long, "Posing problems that would cross / The rabbi's eyes." This is how a treasure story is supposed to be told.

Abba Judah

Now there was a certain man there, by the name of Abba Judah. He would fulfill the commandment [of supporting the sages] in a liberal spirit. One time he lost all his money, and he saw our rabbis and despaired [of helping them]. He went home, and his face was filled with suffering. His wife said to him, "Why is your face filled with suffering?" He said to her, "Our rabbis are here, and I simply do not know what I can do for them." His wife, who was even more righteous than he, said to him, "You have a single field left. Go and sell half of it and give the proceeds to them." He went and did just that. He came to our rabbis, and he gave them the proceeds.

Our rabbis prayed in his behalf. They said to him, "Abba Judah, may the Holy One, blessed be He, make up all the things you lack." When they went their way, he went down to plow the half-field that remained in his possession. Now while he was ploughing in the half-field that remained to him, his only cow fell and broke a leg. He went down to bring her up, and the Holy One, blessed be He, opened his eyes, and he found a jewel. He said, "It was for my own good that my cow broke its leg."

Now when our rabbis returned, they asked about him. They said, "How are things with Abba Judah?" People replied, "Who can even gaze upon the face of Abba Judah — Abba Judah of the oxen! Abba Judah of the camels! Abba Judah of the asses!" So Abba Judah had returned to his former wealth. Now he came to our rabbis and asked after their welfare. They said to him, "How is Abba Judah doing?" He said to them, "Your prayer in my behalf has yielded fruit." They said to him, "Even though to begin with other people gave more than you did, you were the one whom we wrote down at the top of the register." They took and seated him with themselves, and they pronounced upon him the following scriptural verse: "A man's gift makes room for him and brings him before great men" (Proverbs 18:16).

Talmud of the Land of Israel, HORAYOT, 3–4

But Jesus's parable story does not move in that direction. The treasure comes first before we find anything out about the man. Is he righteous or unrighteous? The treasure is simply hidden in a field, much like the situation described by Josephus during the siege of

Jerusalem. We don't know how the treasure got there or to whom it belongs.

When the man finds it, his first response is to cover it up again. Then he buys the field.

The Problem

With the buying of the field the problems begin. Interpreters and interpretations divide into two camps: those who think what the man did was right and those who think that what he did was wrong. For the first group the parable's point is the sheer joy of finding and for them it illustrates the same pattern as the Proverbs poem. For those who think that what the man did was wrong, there arise many problems of interpretation.

So, was the man's action right or wrong?

The legal evidence is not clear. Since the parable compresses a larger story into such a small space, important details are left out. For example, in selling the field, did the owner specify that it was to be sold with moveable property or not. This makes a difference. If it was sold with moveable property, then the man's actions might appear to be legal.

Yet other questions might be asked. The rabbis divide found goods into two groups. Goods that show some evidence of an owner must be brought forward and made public. For example, if you find coins just scattered about on the road, you can keep them. Why? Because they show no evidence of ownership. But if the coins are stacked up, they show evidence of ownership, and so must be made public. By this rule, the man who found the hidden treasure should make it public and available to be claimed.

Another story from the *Talmud* illustrates the problem. In this story Alexander the Great visits the king of Qasya. According to the account in the *Talmud*, Alexander has come to see how the king distributes alms — always a major rabbinic concern — and how he makes decisions.

In this story the seller maintains that the treasure belongs to the buyer and the buyer maintains it belongs to the seller. This suggests that the legal situation is not exactly clear, and furthermore it demonstrates the righteousness of both seller and buyer. The king employs a Solomon-like decision by having the children of the two marry, thus avoiding the problem. Alexander the Great proposes the royal decision, in which the government claims all. Such royal prerogative, by the way, did not hold in the Roman Empire.

Alexander the Great and the King of Qasya

While he was chatting with him, someone came with a case against his fellow. He had bought a piece of a field with its rubbish dump, and he had found a trove of money in it. The one who had bought the property said, "I bought a junk pile; a trove I didn't buy." The one who had sold the property said, "A junk pile and everything in it is what I sold you." While they were arguing with one another, the king said to one of them, "Do you have a male child?" He said to him, "Yes." He said to his fellow, "Do you have a female child?" He said to him, "Yes." He said to them, "Let this one marry that one, and let the treasure-trove belong to the two of them." [Alexander] began to laugh. He said to him, "Now why are you laughing? Didn't I judge the case properly?" He said to him, "If such a case came before you, how would you have judged it?" He said to him, "We should have killed both this one and that one, and kept the treasure for the king."

Talmud of the Land of Israel, BABA MEZIA, 2.6

While it may it be that in Jesus' treasure parable the situation is not perfectly clear, the parable itself gives us the decisive clue, especially in the comparison with the behavior of the two men in the story of Alexander the Great. If the treasure belongs to the man plowing the field, then there is no reason for him to buy the field. But if the treasure does not belong to him, then there is no justification for him to hide the treasure and buy the field. What he has done is unjust, as his very actions disclose to us. Those who insist that the accent is on the joy of the finder, and argue that his actions are either proper or excusable, reduce the ethics of the situation to "finders keepers, losers weepers."

Hidden Treasure

The <Father's> Imperial rule is like a man who had a treasure hidden in a field but did not know it. And when he died he left it to his son. The son did not know <about it either>. He took over the field

and sold it. The buyer went plowing, discovered the treasure, and began to lend money at interest to whomever he wished.
    THOMAS 109

The treasure parable in the Gospel of Thomas avoids the ethical problem by making the finder of the treasure three generations removed and legal owner of the field, so there can be no question of his right to the treasure. I am almost convinced that the Thomas tradition at some point knew the tradition that ends up in Matthew. I don't think he knew the Gospel of Matthew, but the oral tradition prior to Matthew. In order to avoid the problem implicit in the Matthew parable, in the Thomas version the first two owners are ignorant of the treasure and the man buys it *before* finding the treasure. Oddly, in Thomas the finder begins to lend money at interest, something on which Thomas frowns. "If you have money, don't lend it at interest. Rather, give [it] to someone from whom you won't get it back' (Thomas 95). The Thomas parable has little likelihood of being one of Jesus' parables. Rather, it is more likely a response to the Jesus parable about Hidden Treasure that seeks to avoid the problems the Jesus parable creates for the hearer.

Hiding and finding

What are we to make of Jesus' Treasure parable? A quick review of the parable suggests a direction. The following translation is very literal and respects the Greek word order.

1. It is like treasure hidden in the field,
2. Which after finding a man **HID**
3. And from sheer joy **GOES**
4. And **SELLS** everything he has
5. And **BUYS** that field.

The initial line introduces the theme of hidden treasure, and the action is dominated by four verbs, the first of which is in a past tense (line 2) and the final three in the present tense (lines 3–5). This construction ties the finding (a participle) with the hiding (aorist verb) as though they were a single activity. The verbs then shift to the present tense to describe the ongoing result of finding/hid. Lines 2 and 3, with the verbs at the end of the line, form a unit that balances lines 4 and 5, with verbs at the beginning of the line. Thus finding/hid and joy/goes are tied together and sells/buys are tied together. The parable's construction makes it clear that the man finds the treasure and without a thought hides it in the field. That is just the way the man is. His joy is a description of his automatic reaction to his good luck. He does not reflect on the right or wrongness of what he does. The narrative of the parable and its compression simply drive on to selling and buying. But the hearer reflects on what's happening.

The parable is not about finding treasure, but finding treasure is about the empire of God. Treasure is normally a metaphor for God's blessing as a reward for a righteous life. This parable is a brilliant image of seduction. The hidden treasure, which should be a reward for good deeds, seduces the man without his thinking into a course of action that has an immoral outcome. Strangely, this same dynamic seduces all those interpreters who think the point of the story is the joy, who attempt to explain away his act or ignore it. In their joy, they want to overlook what is actually happening.

Robert Duvall's film *The Apostle* (1998) exposes this fault line in religion. Sonny Dewey (aka the Apostle) is absolutely convinced of his call from God. He is a Holy Ghost preacher, brilliantly portrayed by Robert Duvall. Sonny is not an Elmer Gantry character. He is neither self-serving nor a con artist. He believes in what he preaches and helps others live lives of genuine virtue. But he himself cannot live up to the standards he preaches. His call seduces him into blindness to his own moral faults.

In compressed form the parable provides a warning: finding treasure can create a joy that seduces us into an action that is heedless of its consequences. Ironically those interpreters who insist that it is not the man' behavior but his joy that counts have been dazzled by an equally false treasure.

7

Samarítan

Samarítan

This fellow was on his way from Jerusalem down to Jericho
    when he fell into the hands of robbers.
They stripped him,
    beat him up,
    and went off,
    leaving him half dead.
Now by coincidence a priest was going down that road;
    when he caught sight of him,
    he went out of his way to avoid him.
In the same way, when a Levite came to the place,
    he took one look at him
    and crossed the road to avoid him.
But this Samaritan who was traveling that way
    came to where he was
    and was moved to pity at the sight of him.
He went up to him
    and bandaged his wounds,
    pouring olive oil and wine on them.
He hoisted him onto his own animal,
    brought him to an inn,
    and looked after him.
The next day he took out two silver coins,
    which he gave to the innkeeper,
    and said,
"Look after him,
    and on my way back I'll reimburse you for any extra
    expense you have had."
        LUKE 10:30–35

The parable of the Good Samaritan is perhaps the most famous of all parables. "Good Samaritan" has even entered the English language and merits a dictionary entry. The *American Heritage Dictionary* defines a Good Samaritan as "A compassionate person who unselfishly helps others." The dictionary article then makes reference to the passage in Luke 10:30–37. We give Samaritan awards to citizens who show special regard for their neighbors and hospitals are often named "Good Samaritan." So this parable has made a deep impression on us.

The principal reason for that deep impression is that the parable of the Samaritan has a surprising hero and we all love hero stories. Two of the most important tales in the western tradition are hero stories. The Iliad is about the great Greek hero Achilles and his eventual slaying of the Trojan hero Hector. The Odyssey takes it name from its hero, Odysseus, and tells the tale of his struggles to return home after the Trojan war and reclaim his kingdom of Ithaca.

The attraction of the Samaritan is that he is an everyday hero, not someone like Achilles or Odysseus, but someone like us. Yet he is a surprising hero because normally Jews and Samaritans were enemies. We like hero stories because they allow us to play hero, to imagine ourselves as other than we normally are, to be greater and more noble than we really are. Hero stories encourage us to better things.

The Good Samaritan

Luke has cast the parable of the Samaritan in his gospel as an example story, one which presents an example of how we should behave. Of all the gospel authors, Luke is the most clever and creative in incorporating the parables into his gospel narrative. It is very difficult to separate them from their Lucan contexts, and many think the effort is not worth it. But several clues indicate that this parable originally circulated in the oral tradition apart from its context in Luke.

The question about the most important commandment (Luke 10:25–28), which introduces the Samaritan story, also occurs in Mark 12:28–34 where the Shema is combined with the command to love your neighbor as yourself. In Mark, Jesus answers and commends the scribe who asked the question for agreeing with his answer, "You are not far from God's domain." In Luke's version, the scribe answers and Jesus agrees, whereupon the scribe asks him to define "neighbor." What is important about this as far as the parable of the Samaritan is concerned is that it shows that the parable and its context are not necessarily connected, that actually the connection is the result of Luke's editorial effort. On the basis of the Two Source Theory, we understand that Luke derived his question from Mark.

Furthermore, the parable is not seamlessly related to the question. The question asked by the lawyer is "Who is my neighbor," whereas the parable, even as Luke himself attests, answers the question "who proved to be my neighbor." So obviously the parable and the question of the definition of neighbor are separate and separable.

What, then, is the parable about?

Jericho

There is a fountain by Jericho, that runs plentifully, and is very fit for watering the ground; it arises near the old city, . . This fountain, at the beginning, . . . was entirely of a sickly and corruptive nature to all things whatsoever; but that it was made gentle, and very wholesome and fruitful, by the prophet Elisha. . . . And that water, which had been the occasion of barrenness and famine before, from that time did supply a numerous posterity, and afforded great abundance to the country. Accordingly, the power of it is so great in watering the ground, that if it do but once touch a country, it affords a sweeter nourishment than other waters do, when they lie so long upon them, till they are satiated with them. . . . There are in it many sorts of palm trees that are watered by it, different from each other in taste and name; the better sort of them, when they are pressed, yield an excellent kind of honey, . . . so that he who should pronounce this place to be divine would not be mistaken, wherein is such plenty of trees produced as are very rare, and of the most excellent sort. And indeed, if we speak of those other fruits, it will not be easy to light on any climate in the habitable earth that can well be compared to it, . . . The ambient air is here also of so good a temperature, that the people of the country are clothed in linen only, even when snow covers the rest of Judea. This place is one hundred and fifty furlongs from Jerusalem, and sixty from Jordan. The country, as far as Jerusalem, is desert and stony; but that as far as Jordan and the lake Asphaltitis lies lower indeed, though it be equally desert and barren. But so much shall suffice to have said about Jericho, and of the great happiness of its situation.

JOSEPHUS, *Jewish Wars*, 4.8.3

Jerusalem to Jericho

This is the only parable that takes place in a specific place, on the road between Jerusalem and Jericho. Most parables are set in a general situation, a field, a house, etc. Also the characters in this parable are specified with greater detail than normal, a priest, a Levite and a Samaritan. Such specification clearly underlines the parable's Jewishness.

Jerusalem is in the hill country (2,700 feet above sea level), while Jericho is on a plain (820 feet below sea level). Jericho as described by Josephus is a beautiful country, well irrigated and lush, called the "City of a Thousand Palms." But the surrounding area is desert. King Herod had a winter palace there and many priests had their homes in Jericho.

The trip down from Jerusalem to Jericho passes through a deserted area, where there are many caves in which to hide. The road was notorious for bandits and one of the unusual aspects of this parable is all the people traveling alone on this road. Normally, folks traveled this route in caravans for protection.

The man falls among robbers who strip him, beat him and leave him half dead. Each of these items calls for comment. In the context of Jesus' story telling we should assume that the man is a Jew, otherwise there should be some specific marker of his identity. If he is stripped, the audience will have no notion of his social class, something clearly marked off by clothing in the ancient world. By being stripped, he truly becomes anonymous.

Left half-dead has provoked a wide range of discussion among commentators. Does this term mean that the man could pass for dead, looks as if he is dead; or that he is near death, clearly in need of help or he will die. The evidence for its meaning is not perfectly clear, so we will work out the possibilities for both cases. An example of the word from 4 Maccabees suggests that it means he is near death.

Half Dead

[10] And while Apollonius was going up with his armed forces to seize the money, angels on horseback with lightning flashing from their weapons appeared from heaven, instilling in them great fear and trembling. [11] *Then Apollonius fell down half dead* in the temple area that was open to all, stretched out his hands toward heaven, and with tears begged the Hebrews to pray for him and propitiate the wrath of the

heavenly army. [12] For he said that he had committed a sin deserving of death, and that if he were spared he would praise the blessedness of the holy place before all people.

4 MACCABEES 4:10–12

Given the man's situation, abandoned and dying in the ditch, the hearer is clued in as to the story's type. We await the arrival of the hero with whom we can identify.

Priest and Levite

First down the road comes a priest, who sees him and passes by. The story describes his action in two verbs. He sees the man in the ditch. It's not just a glance. The Greek verb describing his action after he sees the man is made up of two prepositions and a verb — literally in English, he passes beside and over and against. The "over and against" is a storyteller's gesture of pushing away.

What was the priest's obligation? Was he required to stop or was he justified in passing on. To some degree it depends upon how we understand "half-dead." If the priest thinks he is dealing with a corpse, he might calculate that he must avoid it, for otherwise he would suffer impurity. According the command in Leviticus, a priest is not allowed to touch a corpse. But in the *Mishnah* and *Talmud* there are extended discussions on this verse, making finer and finer gradations all to the point that if the corpse is abandoned, that takes precedence over the Leviticus rule. Taking care of an abandoned corpse takes precedence even over studying the Torah. But then again, all these fine distinctions stem from learned discussions of the rabbis,

Priests and Corpses

He shall not go where there is a dead body; he shall not defile himself even for his father or mother.

LEVITICUS 21.11

A high priest or a Nazarite may not contact uncleanness because of their [dead] kindred, but they may contact uncleanness because of a neglected corpse. If they were on a journey and found a neglected corpse, R. Eliezer says: The high priest may contact uncleanness but the Nazarite may not contact uncleanness.

Mishnah NAZIR, 7.1 (DANBY)

so a priest, who follows the strict construction of the Torah, might set them aside as just liberal reductions of the Torah's true meaning. If on the other hand "half-dead" means that the man is close to death, then the priest's duty is clear. He must come to the man's aid.

Perhaps the priest has other very legitimate concerns. Maybe the man in the ditch is only a decoy for robbers who will attack him when he stops to help. So he prudently rushes on past the man in the ditch.

In the end, all these speculations are useless. The storyteller provides no reason for the priest's action. He just acts that way. Perhaps the storyteller shares the common anti-clericalism of the day. This is just the way priests are. At any rate, the storyteller is uninterested in the priest's motives and simply describes his actions.

This same scenario is repeated in the case of the Levite. The Levite and the priest belong to the same tribe of Levi, but the priests are descendents of Aaron. Since Levites were employed in regular temple service, we could rehearse the same set of excuses, but the storyteller is uninterested. These two members of the religious elite simply pass on by on the other side.

Samaritan

A first century Jewish audience now knows what is going to happen next in this hero story. The third character will be one of them, an Israelite, meaning a Jewish layperson. The expected triad is priest, Levite and Israelite. As the great Jewish scholar Claude Montifiore once remarked, the triad in this parable "is no less queer and impossible than 'Priest, Deacon, and Frenchman' would be to us today" (vol. 2, p. 467). The expected English triad would be priest, deacon and layman. The ancient world was extremely hierarchical and these hierarchies were well known to all. The *Mishnah* provides a good example of hierarchical arrangement and the expected triad.

Triad
A priest takes precedence over a Levite, a Levite over an Israelite, and Israelite over a *mamzer* [bastard], a *mamzer* over a *Netin* [temple slave], a *Netin* over a proselyte, a proselyte over a freed slave."
Mishnah HORAYOT, 3:8 (NEUSNER)

But instead of the expected Israelite, the hated Samaritan makes an appearance. The origin of the animosity between Jews and Samaritans is probably lost in the dark shadows of history, but by the time of Jesus, the hostility was well established. It appears to involve a division about where to worship (Jerusalem for Jews, and Mount Gerizim for the Samaritans) and two different versions of the Pentateuch. The Samaritans claimed that the Jewish Torah had been redacted so as to eliminate the true worship on Mount Gerizim, while of course Jews claimed the opposite. About 500 Samaritans continue to live near the West Bank town of Nablus, which is in the shadow of Mount Gerizim. For Jews at Jesus' time the Samaritans were foreigners (see Luke 17:18).

A comparison of the description of the three characters who approach the man in the ditch indicates both similarities and differ-

By chance a certain priest	was going down on that **road**	**and upon seeing** him *passed-by-on-the-other-side*
Likewise also a Levite	upon at that place *coming*	**and upon seeing** *passed-by-on-the-other-side.*
But a certain Samaritan	while on the road *came* upon him	**and upon seeing** had compassion

ences. The table is a literal translation of Greek representing its word order and phonetic similarities.

The priest and the Levite are clearly viewed in parallel, with the accent on the final, verb "passed-by-on-the-other-side." The second column indicates how the description of the Samaritan's approach is made up of words from the descriptions both the priest and Levite: "road" and "coming". This similarity would lead an audience to expect the Samaritan would behave just the same as the priest and Levite. When the Samaritan "came upon him" the Greek may imply that the man's approach entailed a threat. In the third column the final action is initiated in exactly the same way, "and upon seeing." This stresses the seeing of the half-dead man in the ditch. It also reinforces the audience's expectation that the Samaritan will behave in at least a similar fashion, if not worse.

Thus the audience is totally unprepared for the final action. The

Samaritan had compassion, took pity on him. The Greek for compassion here refers to the entrails, which for the ancients was the seat of the emotions, somewhat like the English "the heart." Perhaps it would be better to translate the phrase, "his heart was moved."

Even though technically only half the story has been told, it is for all practical purposes over. The Samaritan's compassion ends the story. There will be no Israelite coming down the road to rescue the half-dead man. This is the only narrative parable in which the punch line occurs in the middle and not the end. Why? I would suggest the continuation of the story allows a hearer time to adjust to the story.

The Samaritan cares for the man's wounds with oil and wine, bandages him up and takes him to an inn. He tells the innkeeper to take care of the man and promises on his return to pay him whatever more is needed.

Identification with the characters is an important element in a story. When the man is attacked and left in the ditch for half-dead, an audience recognizes this as a hero story and awaits arrival of the hero, with whom they will identify. In a very real sense, they will ride to the rescue of the man in the ditch. When the Samaritan first approaches, this plan remains in force and is even reinforced by the similarity of his description to those of the priest and Levite, failed heroes. But when he has compassion, this plan is thrown into a cocked hat. A hearer has three options.

"In real life this would never happen. It's only a story, fiction."

Such a person has forfeited the parable's opportunity of envisioning life anew. Such people remain in the same old world in which they have always dwelt. This is almost always the response of the literal minded, who refuse the option of imagination.

A second option is to identify with the Samaritan.

For a hearer who wants to remain in the hero's role, that is the only alternative. For some few in Jesus' audience this may have been an option. But such people are already different and do not live by the normal values of the Palestinian world of the first century.

Finally, a hearer can identify with the man in the ditch.

If we want to stay in the parable and experience a new world, that is our only available choice. Having begun the parable in expectation of playing the role of the hero, one ends in the role of the victim, being taken care of by one's mortal and moral enemy. The parable announces that the savior is a Samaritan — the hated one.

We should be careful not to underestimate the difficulty of this final option. I would assume that most people in Jesus' audience opted for number one: it's only a story; in reality it would never have happened.

It's always a question how much one should play with a story, how much imagination is licensed by the story, but surely this one suggests that we at least experiment with it. As one begins to play with the story, it appears strange that no one asks the man in the ditch whether he wants the Samaritan to take care of him. He might well want to take his chances and wait for an Israelite. Surely there must be one coming down this road, since one of everything else has.

What if the Samaritan betrays him? What if he turns on him and kills him or sells him into slavery? After all he is a Samaritan. And what about the inn? Inns in the ancient world were not Holiday Inns. Inns and innkeepers had very dubious reputations.

The Samaritan says that he will return, at least to pay the inn-keeper whatever extra is owed for the man's upkeep. Does this imply that the Samaritan expects to visit the man? How is the man to explain these events to his family and his neighbors? Will he be forced to introduce the Samaritan to his family?

Well, maybe we have gone too far, but it does make evident that the man has problems. He surely would prefer an Israelite. There would be less to explain.

Rabbinic parable

In fairness to the priest and Levite, the following wonderful rabbinic tale perhaps tells the tale from their point of view.

Rabbi Nahum's Tale

It is related of Nahum of Gamzu that he was blind in both his eyes, his two hands and legs were amputated, and his whole body was covered with boils and he was lying in a dilapidated house on a bed the feet of which were standing in bowls of water in order to prevent the ants from crawling on to him; . . . his disciples said to him, Master, since you are wholly righteous, why has all this befallen you? And he replied, I have brought it all upon myself. Once I was journeying on the road and was making for the house of my father-in-law and I had with me three asses, one laden with food, one with drink and one with all kinds of dainties, when a poor man met me and stopped me on the road and said to me, "Master, give me something to eat." I replied to him, "Wait until I have unloaded something from the ass;" I had hardly managed to unload one thing from the ass when the man died [from hunger]. I then went and laid myself on him and exclaimed, "May my eyes which had no pity upon your eyes become blind, may my hands which had no pity upon your hands be cut off, may my legs be amputated, and my mind was not at rest until I added, may my whole body be covered with boils." Thereupon his pupils exclaimed, "Alas! that we see you in such a sore plight." To this he replied, "Woe would it be to me did you not see me in such a sore plight."

Babylonian Talmud, TAANITH 21.A (SONCINO)

Rabbi Nahum's state is extreme, but its parallel to the parable of the Samaritan is interesting. Both take place on a journey, both involve helping someone in need. Rabbi Nahum regrets his action for the rest of his life. His tale is a strong reminder of the injunction to help the other. It is a good example of the answer to the question, "Who is my neighbor?" Its point of view is that of the helper, the hero to be, the rescuer.

Jesus' parable takes a slightly different point of view. Its point of view is that of the victim, the one in need of help. It proposes a new world in which the wall between *us* and *them* no longer exists and even more that one of *them* can come to the aid of *us*.

There is another way to imagine this parable. Shakespeare's *Romeo and Juliet* is the same story but with the *us/them* still firmly in place. When Romeo and Juliet step across the line between the Capulets and the Montagues, no one else from either family follows. And so the tragedy plays out its inevitable end in the deaths of the two young lovers. This comparison to *Romeo and Juliet* points out that Jesus' parable and Shakespeare's play are not about individuals, but communities. Not just individuals have to cross the line, but communities have to cross the line. Yet the crossing of that line always begins with the first Samaritan whose heart is moved by a Jew. Such people are initiating a new world for all of us.

8

The Prodigals

The Prodigals

Once there was this man who had two sons.
The younger of them said to his father,
   "Father, give me the share of the property that's coming to me."
So he divided his resources between them.
Not too many days later, the younger son got all his things
together
   and left home for a faraway country,
   where he squandered his property by living extravagantly.
   Just when he had spent it all,
   a serious famine swept through that country,
   and he began to do without.
So he went
   and hired himself out to one of the citizens of that country,
      who sent him out to his farm to feed the pigs.
   He longed to satisfy his hunger with the carob pods,
      which the pigs usually ate;
   but no one offered him anything.
Coming to his senses he said,
   "Lots of my father's hired hands have more than enough to eat,
      while here I am dying of starvation!
   I'll get up and go to my father
   and I'll say to him,
   'Father,
      I have sinned against heaven and affronted you;
      I don't deserve to be called a son of yours any longer;
      treat me like one of your hired hands.'"
   And he got up and returned to his father.
But while he was still a long way off,
   his father caught sight of him

and was moved to compassion.
He went running out to him,
threw his arms around his neck,
and kissed him
and the son said to him,
"Father,
    I have sinned against heaven and affronted you;
    I don't deserve to be called a son of yours any longer."
But the father said to his slaves,
"Quick!
Bring out the finest robe and put it on him;
put a ring on his finger
and sandals on his feet.
Fetch the fat calf and slaughter it;
let's have a feast and celebrate,
    because this son of mine was dead
    and has come back to life;
    he was lost
    and now is found."
And they started celebrating.
Now his elder son was out in the field;
  and as he got closer to the house,
  he heard music and dancing.
He called one of the servant-boys over
  and asked what was going on.
He said to him,
"Your brother has come home
and your father has slaughtered the fat calf,
    because he has him back safe and sound."
But he was angry
  and refused to go in.
So his father came out
  and began to plead with him.
But he answered his father,
"See here,
  all these years I have slaved for you.
  I never once disobeyed any of your orders;
  yet you never once provided me with a kid goat
    so I could celebrate with my friends.
  But when this son of yours shows up,
    the one who has squandered your estate with prostitutes —
for him you slaughter the fat calf."
But (the father) said to him,
"My child,
  you are always at my side.
  Everything that's mine is yours.

But we just had to celebrate and rejoice,
because this brother of yours was dead,
    and has come back to life;
he was lost,
    and now is found."
    LUKE 15:11–32

Next to the parable of the Samaritan, the parable of the Prodigals or the Father and Two Sons is one of the most popular and frequently quoted. It often appears in stained glass windows and artwork. Yet both the traditional title and the history of art indicate that emphasis has fallen on the first part, the story of the prodigal son. Seldom in the artwork is there even an image of the elder son. He has almost disappeared.

The parable occurs only in the Gospel of Luke where it is cast with two other parables, the Lost Sheep and the Lost Coin. The key word combination of lost sheep, lost coin, lost son ties the section together. Furthermore, Luke has set the parable in a context in which toll collectors and sinners are coming to Jesus, and Jesus' opponents complain. "Now the toll collectors and sinners kept crowding around Jesus so they could hear him. But the Pharisees and the scholars would complain to each other: 'This fellow welcomes sinners and eats with them'" (Luke 15:1–2). "Complain" is also used in a parallel passage in Luke 19:7 in the story of Zaccahaus, the head toll collector. Seeing Zacchaeus high up in his tree, Jesus tells him to come down because "I have to stay at your house today" (Luke 19:5). But the crowd begins to protest. "Everyone who saw this complained: 'He is going to spend the day with some sinner!'" (verse 7).

Both of these verses echo the famous passage in Numbers 14 when the people complain against Moses and Aaron before they begin the invasion of the Land of Canaan.

> And all the Israelites complained against Moses and Aaron; the whole congregation said to them, "Would that we had died in the land of Egypt! Or would that we had died in this wilderness! Why is the LORD bringing us into this land to fall by the sword?"
> NUMBERS 14:2–3

In both these passages Luke echoes this famous story because he is trying to draw a parallel between the people of Israel then — during the time of Moses — and now — during the time of Jesus. Just as they rejected Moses and Aaron, so they are rejecting Jesus.

In this context the first two parables, the Lost Sheep and the Lost Coin, are examples of sinners being welcomed. The tag attached to each of the two makes this clear: "I'm telling you it'll be just like this in heaven: there'll be more celebrating over one sinner who has a change of heart than over ninety-nine virtuous people who have no need to change their hearts" (Luke 15:7 and also 10). The final parable extends this example further with the elder son serving as a representative of those who complain against eating with sinners. This complex of parables, cleverly situated by Luke, is part of his overall pattern to demonstrate the rejection of Israel in favor of the church.

The image of protesting Pharisees has convinced many that Luke has got it right. As the famous parable scholar Joachim Jeremias notes:

> The parable was addressed to men who were like the elder brother, men who were offended at the gospel . . . His hearers were in the position of the elder son who had to decide whether he would accept his father's invitation and share his joy. So Jesus does not yet pronounce sentence; he still has hope of moving them to abandon their resistance to the gospel, he still hopes that they will recognize how their self-righteousness and lovelessness separate them from God, and that they may come to experience the great joy which the Good News brings (p. 131–32).

But there's a rub. The parable doesn't quite make the point Jeremias and Luke think it should. Why should they repent and believe in the gospel if, as the father says at the parable's end, "you are always at my side. Everything that's mine is yours." Furthermore, there is no evidence that Jesus' vision involved a rejection of God's chosen people.

So we must try again to understand the parable. What clues does it offer us?

This parable is by far the longest in the Jesus tradition and is also long by rabbinic standards, although there are rabbinic parables that equal it in length. We might want to take this length seriously and realize that Jesus here is pushing the boundaries of parable. Parables work by compression, and while this one has its share of compression, it demands that we track three characters and a variety of scene changes. The parable's length has led to debates as to exactly how to divide it. Some see two parts, the first dealing with the younger son and the second the elder.

- Younger Son (13–24)
- Elder Son (25–32)

Still others see a division into three parts.

- Younger son (13–20)
- Father's Response (21–24)
- Elder Son (25–32)

Both divisions have their advantages, and since the parable was originally performed out loud and not printed, an exact division is probably not necessary. The first schema sees two stories, that of the two boys, while the second follows the character who is controlling the story. Neither quite works because such divisions are the result of the printing press. The ear hears in a continuous line, while the eye divides. Print likes sharp divisions; the ear prefers seamless transitions.

Sibling rivalry

A King and Two Sons

R. Berechiah said in the name of R. Jonathan: . . . The verse means therefore that God has set love of little children in their fathers' hearts. For example, there was a king who had two sons, one grown up, the other a little one. The grown-up one was scrubbed clean, and the little one was covered with dirt, but the king loved the little one more than he loved the grown-up one.

Midrash ON PSALMS, 9

Like the little parable of R. Berechiah, the Prodigals is an ancient tale of sibling favoritism. Such tales are inherent in family structure and all cultures have them. The play and film *Amadeus (1984)*, a story of intrigue and hate between the older, less talented Antonio Salieri and the younger and profligate Mozart, is a recent reincarnation of this tale. The beautiful film *A River Runs Through It* (1992) tells the same story about the hard working elder brother and the wastrel younger son, born to be a fly fisherman. As we might suspect, the younger son is the apple of his father and mother's eye.

At some fundamental level such stories move us because they are true. They tell us about family life, the loves and rivalries that tear it apart.

Parables compress, as we should remember even in this long parable. In this story of family life, the family has been compressed to a father and two sons. Missing are the mother and sisters and, given the size of ancient families, other brothers. We should not imagine this as an American nuclear family. Possibly the father and elder son are closer in age than the two sons. Nor need the sons be the children of the same mother. As the parable develops this is a family of some wealth, not an ordinary peasant family. They have enough land to send the younger son off for a grand adventure, slaves and hired hands, and most importantly, a fatted calf.

The parable begins with the simple line "this man . . .had two sons." While simple enough it hides or implies a great deal. Family relations in the ancient world were very different from our own. Fathers were remote and figures of authority. They did not normally have relations of intimacy with their own children. The elder son's complaint that he has slaved for his father all these years is one most sons would have made against their fathers. Fathers almost literally owned their children. They gave and received in marriage, and could deal with them as they saw fit.

When the parable begins with "this man had two sons" it's not just an observation of biological relation; it's stating a social fact. He owns the boys and determines their fates.

Request and inheritance

When the younger son comes and asks the father for his share of the inheritance, it appears to us innocent and worthy of admiration. The boy is showing initiative and seems ready to make his way in the world, to seek his fortune. But the ancients would have viewed this much differently. They would have seen it as an attack on the father, a violation of the commandment to honor your father and mother. In their view the son is asking his father to drop dead. In the Greek text of the parable this is made evident, although all translations avoid the point. The following word for word translation makes the point clear.

> Father,
> Give to me the belongs-to-me part of the substance (*ousia*).
> And he divided among them his life (*bios*)

The son's request and the father's response would have appalled an ancient audience. Why?

Sirach sums up the common wisdom. It is a stain against your honor to make yourself dependent on you children. While you "have breath in you" don't do it. Sirach's advice is clear. "In the hour of death, distribute your inheritance."

Advice on Inheritance

²⁰ To son or wife, to brother or friend,
do not give power over yourself, as long as you live;
and do not give your property to another,
in case you change your mind and must ask for it.
²¹ While you are still alive and have breath in you,
do not let anyone take your place.
²² For it is better that your children should ask from you
than that you should look to the hand of your children.
²³ Excel in all that you do;
bring no stain upon your honor.
²⁴ At the time when you end the days of your life,
in the hour of death, distribute your inheritance.
Sirach 33:20–24

If Sirach warns against what the father does, the case law is equally clear against this situation. The beginning of the case law is Deuteronomy 21. This is a remarkable text, especially given what is not in our parable. The elder son is to get two thirds of the property, and the younger son (and any other sons) can divide the other third among themselves. The point of this case law is to protect the family, not the individual. The family's survival is what counts. The elder son who controls two-thirds of the property can then buy out the younger sons and maintain the family possessions. To be a younger son was a condemnation to poverty, or near poverty. This situation held true for a long time, as the readers of Jane Austen's novels will recognize. In her tales, the plot frequently turns on the lack of an inheritance.

¹⁵ If a man has two wives, one of them loved and the other disliked, and if both the loved and the disliked have borne him sons, the firstborn being the son of the one who is disliked, ¹⁶ then on the day when he wills his possessions to his sons, he is not permitted to treat the son of the loved as the firstborn in preference to the son of the disliked, who is the firstborn. ¹⁷ He must acknowledge as firstborn the

son of the one who is disliked, giving him a double portion of all that
he has; since he is the first issue of his virility, the right of the firstborn
is his.

DEUTERONOMY 21:15–17

The case law in Deuteronomy reflects a very real situation in which
the father in old age marries a young woman and favors her children.
The story of Jacob, his favorite wife Rachael and her son Joseph follows this narrative line. But more on that later.

The parable speaks the truth when it describes the father as divid-
ing his life between them. He has died for his children and would be
judged by an ancient audience as a fool. A rabbinic proverb declares
that among those who cry out to God and can expect no answer is
"he who transfers his property to his children in his lifetime"
(*Babylonian Talmud*, BABA MEZIA, 75B).

Departure and fall

So against all wisdom and advice, the father divides his property,
the son converts his share into cash and departs for a faraway country. Much is left unsaid at this point. It's not clear from the case law
how we are to imagine this situation. Normally the property could
not be converted to cash until the father had died and the mother and
sisters provided for. But like much that happens in parables, the form
allows the teller of the tale to skip over the details and get to the
essentials. The boy takes off.

By faraway land it does not have to mean "really" far away. We
need not imagine the younger son like some younger English son
going off to the far reaches of the Empire to make his wealth. In
Galilee, a faraway town could be just over the hill in one of the gentile cities. Since the elder son appears to know what his younger
brother is up to, this one can't be too far away.

The son's first act of requesting his share of the inheritance implies
that he wants his father to drop dead. This creates our initial view of
him and he continues to live up to his advanced billing. He immediately throws away all his money. He did not lose it in bad invest-
ments. No, he squandered it in extravagant living. The Greek word
(*asotos*) has the sense of profligate with a hint of sexual excess
implied. Now all of his inheritance is gone. How quickly this plot
degenerates!

The scourge of the ancient world, a famine, suddenly makes his fate yet worse. Famine served as a population control mechanism and was a constant threat. To those who were landless, famine and starvation were always lurking around the corner. Now the younger son has joined those who are at risk.

He hires himself out to one of the citizens of that country, that is, a gentile. Now he belongs with the foreigners. How far he has traveled from his family! How far he has fallen! But he has yet further to fall. That citizen sends him out to his farm to feed the pigs. At this point the boy has committed apostasy. He has not only drifted far from his family but also from Torah. Leviticus clearly marks out the pig as unclean, to be avoided (see also Deuteronomy 14:8). So characteristic is Jewish avoidance of pigs that in the martyrdom of Eleazar he is forced to eat pork. He would rather die than submit. So the young man's feeding swine marks him out as having abandoned the traditions of his ancestors.

He is so low that he would even share the food of pigs. As the old saying has it, he is so low he can reach up and touch bottom. The plot needs a new direction.

The Greek text simply says, "He came to himself." Some have tried to see in this a reference to Christian repentance, but that seems unlikely for several reasons.

- The phrase simply means he came to his senses.
- The boy shows no signs of repentance. He just wants to get out of the predicament he is in. He is destitute.
- If Luke thought it meant repentance, why not use that word, especially since it is a favorite theme of Luke's.
- St. Augustine in his comment on this parable does not interpret the boy's action as repentance.

Pigs

[7] The pig, . . . even though it has divided hoofs and is cleft-footed, . . . does not chew the cud; it is unclean for you. [8] Of their flesh you shall not eat, and their carcasses you shall not touch; they are unclean for you.

LEVITICUS 11:7–8

So the younger son formulates a plan. Since his father's hired hands have plenty of food, he will propose to his father that he become a hired hand. What are we to make of his proposal — or, more importantly, what would an ancient audience have made of it? We should remember that his behavior to this point has not been exemplary, so perhaps we should be on our guard. Is he trying to strike a deal, to somehow remain in control? As a hired hand, he will be owed a wage. As a son, he would be dependent on the father. Or, is his proposal entirely sincere? Does he really expect the father to treat him as a hired hand instead of a son? How often in the past has he, the younger, the favorite, gotten away with it? The story doesn't give us the answers, but his behavior certainly suggests the questions.

The plot has now changed; and signaling this, the son rises up from his low position and heads home. The getting up shows just how cleverly this parable is put together. The son is metaphorically at his low point and when the tragic direction of the plot is reversed, he comes to his senses and he gets up. The metaphorical trajectory of the story is matched by the physical actions of rising up and returning home.

Father's response

With the son's return the story's focus shifts to the father. To this point we have been watching the son's actions. Now we turn to watch the father. We first catch a glimpse of him while his son is "still a long way off." It is as though our point of view has shifted to let us look over the father' shoulder. The father catches sight of him just at the point he comes over the horizon. The implication is that the father has been watching for the boy. This is our first hint that the boy will be welcomed back. But from the point of view of the ancient audi-

---

Martyrdom of Eleazar

[18] Eleazar, one of the scribes in high position, a man now advanced in age and of noble presence, was being forced to open his mouth to eat swine's flesh. [19] But he, welcoming death with honor rather than life with pollution, went up to the rack of his own accord, spitting out the flesh, [20] as all ought to go who have the courage to refuse things that it is not right to taste, even for the natural love of life.

2 MACCABEES 6:18–20

ence, such watching would only confirm that the father is still a fool, that he has little honor. As soon as the father sees the son, he has compassion for him. This phrase echoes the same phrase in the parable of the Samaritan. In that parable it cut off an audience's expectation that the Samaritan would do some further dastardly deed to the man in the ditch. The audience was shocked. Compassion in Jesus' parables comes as a shock, as unexpected. Here too an audience has its expectations pulled up short. The father has shown his hand. He will take back the son. But an audience would have expected more of the father.

The Greek text describes the father's action in a series of verbs connected by "and" with the verbal action in the first place.

saw him his father did

and **moved to compassion**

and **running fell** on his neck

and **kissed** him.

The action is presented in a staccato fashion, bang, bang, bang, bang. The picture these verbs create does not flatter the father. They do not add up to a portrait of an honorable oriental gentleman. Older gentlemen of honor do not run except in cases of emergency. To run would mean hiking up his robes so that his legs would show, a disgraceful act. It has been suggested that he is running not so much to welcome the son, but to get to him before the villagers can express their disgust at the son's return.

The father "fell on his neck." This indicates the father is treating the son as at least an equal, since normally, we would expect the son to be falling before the father, whom he has sinned against. Finally, the father kisses him. The Greek verb's prefix seems to represent an intensification, "he kissed him over and over." A good example occurs earlier in Luke in the story of the woman who anoints Jesus. When the woman enters, "Her tears wet his feet, and she wiped them dry with her hair; she kissed his feet, and anointed them with myrrh" (Luke 7:38). When Simon the Pharisee complains about the woman's unsightly behavior, Jesus draws a sharp contrast between their greetings: "You didn't offer me a kiss, but she hasn't stopped kissing my feet since I arrived" (7:45). In both cases the verb describing the woman's activity is the same as is used of the father, while Simon's unoffered "kiss" lacks the intensifying prefix. The father is not offering Simon's kiss of greeting. He is doing more. So perhaps we should imagine the father behaving like the woman kissing Jesus over and over again.

Reception

The son begins his prepared speech, but the father cuts him off before he can finish it. The father is clearly now in charge of this narrative. He gives a series of orders to show the full reinstatement of the son. The finest robe is probably the father's robe, the ring on his finger is a signet ring signifying power and sandals on his feet indicate that he is no longer to go about as a slave, but as a son.

He also commands his slaves to kill the fatted calf and prepare the feast. The fatted calf was an especially important sign of the feast, and since meat had to be eaten when cooked or it would spoil, this indicates that a large party is in progress. The father's welcoming of the son is not just a family affair: it will be publicly announced and celebrated with the village.

Two quick points need to be made.

The father has gone too far. There is no test of the son, no questioning of his motives. This son has behaved in an outrageous fashion, insulted his father, lost the inheritance, committed apostasy. The list could go on and on. The father makes no judgment, demands no price from the son. He is back. No questions asked. Dead and alive. Lost and found.

The son's reception is a dream come true. He has gotten away with it. He sinned against heaven and his father, and he's not going to be punished.

Before we go on to the elder son's part of the story, I think it is

---

A King and his Son

A king had a son who had gone astray from his father a journey of a hundred days; his friends said to him, 'Return to your father;' he said, 'I cannot.' Then his father sent to say, 'Return as far as you can, and I will come to you the rest of the way.' So God says, 'Return to me, and I will return to you.'

Pesikta Rabbati, 184B–185 quoted in *Rabbinic Anthology*, P. 321

important to issue a word of caution. The younger son's story is a favorite of Christian preaching. For many it summarizes the Gospel, the message of a gracious father's forgiving of a wayward child. But this is not just the Christian story, it is more importantly the story of Israel. As the parable of the King makes clear, this is how God has always dealt with his wandering children. It is Christian anti-Semitism that sees this story only as the essence of the Gospel. This story was stolen from Israel.

The younger son's story evokes the universal quality of the need to be restored to innocence. Dag Hammarskjöld catches this sense very clearly.

> Forgiveness is the answer to the child's dream of a miracle by which what is broken is made whole again, what is soiled is again made clean. The dream explains why we need to be forgiven, and why we must forgive. In the presence of God, nothing stands between Him and us — we *are* forgiven. But we *cannot* feel His presence if anything is allowed to stand between ourselves and others (p. 124).

Elder son

As we have seen, younger and elder sons play stereotyped roles. In the parable of the king with two sons with which we opened this section, the younger son is described as "covered with dirt" and the elder "scrubbed clean." Yet "the king loved the little one more than he loved the grown-up one." This describes the expected plot of the story. The younger son of the parable has certainly covered himself with dirt. The father has certainly demonstrated his love of him. Now we expect to see the one scrubbed clean, whom the father will love less.

The elder son is an important man. If we think of the family situation, he should not be viewed as young adult, but a mature, perhaps middle-aged man. He may well be running his father's business and highly respected in the village. He's a hard worker, that's why he's out in the field.

Nor has he been invited to the party. As he comes home he hears music and dancing. He calls a "servant boy" and asks what is happening. The Greek points up an irony: he is an elder (*presbyteros*) of the family, but he calls on the child servant (*pias*) for information. The irony reinforces the hierarchical distinction.

The artifice of the story teller is on exhibit here. When the elder asks the child servant what is going on, the storyteller could have had the servant say, "And he told him." Instead the servant boy summarizes the story from the father's point of view, setting in sharp contrast the elder son outside and the younger son and father inside at the party of the fatted calf, safe and sound.

The elder son's response is immediate and strong. He is angry and refuses to go in. He insults the father, throws down a challenge to his authority and decisions.

The father comes out and instead of confronting the insult, forcing the elder brother to come into the party and accept the father's decision, he pleads with the son to come in. Has this father no honor?

The elder son in response draws a sharp contrast between his behavior and that of the younger son. The elder views himself as his father's slave "for all these years." Never once has he disobeyed any of his commands. In contrast "this son of yours" (not "my brother') has wasted the father's life (*bios*, the term used at the parable's beginning to describe what the father has divided) with whores. "Prostitutes" or " "harlots" the normal English translation is too formal, too polite, for this Greek word.

What has been the father's response to the elder's slaving and obedience? "You never once provided me with a kid goat so I could celebrate with my friends." We already know the younger son's reward — the fatted calf.

The elder son has added insult to injury. Now we expect the father to finally defend his honor, to force the elder son to accept his decision to receive back his younger son.

Father's response

The father's response is totally unexpected. He begins by addressing the *elder* son as "my dear child." He uses a term of real familiarity, of intimacy. This parable has been very careful in its use of terms to describe its characters. In the beginning, the father has two sons, perhaps better translated "male heirs." One is younger, the other elder. Younger and elder spell out specific roles and expectations, both in story and in law. In the elder son's story, he addresses not just a slave or a hired hand, but a boy-servant. The hierarchy of relations is carefully maintained in this parable. But at this critical junction, the father strips away the hierarchy, returns to a term of childhood, almost as though he is treating the elder as a baby.

Furthermore, the father affirms, "you are always at my side. Everything that's mine is yours." This is going to come as a real shock to the younger son. Perhaps it explains the elder's anger. Not only is he upset with the father's refusal to up hold the family honor, but perhaps he is afraid that the son with the best robe, the signet ring and shoes on his feet will somehow become once again an heir — something the father has the power to do if he wishes.

Instead the father has created a dilemma. Inside at the party is a younger son thinking he has gotten away with it, that he has been restored. Outside is an elder brother with all the property, with all the power, and he is angry.

Rivalry

There are several ways to try to put this story together. One is the model we have been following, a story of sibling rivalry. That story formula has worked so far, and clearly the parable derives from that story formula. But in certain important ways the parable varies from expectation. Unlike the king who loves the younger son who is covered with dirt, this father loves both of his sons. There is nothing they can do that will finally insult him. The younger son wants to kill him off and squanders his inheritance; yet the father graciously welcomes him back. The elder son refuses to join the party and accept the father's welcoming of the younger son. The father comes out and tenderly calls him "my dear child."

This parable violates expectations at an even deeper level. Most stories of this type purchase the righteousness of one character at the expense of the other. That is why in classical storytelling we have a protagonist and antagonist. The formula of sibling rivalry clearly sets up the expectation in story that the younger son will play the role of protagonist and the elder the antagonist. Luke attempts to fit the parable into such a frame by identifying the sinners/"Lost Sheep" with the younger son and the complainers with the Pharisees and the elder son. But that does not happen here. The father clearly accepts the elder son. "You are always at my side. Everything that's mine is yours." In this story neither son gets the better of the other. Actually, they are the antagonists and the father is protagonist. Yet he reconciles them to himself. Nothing they do can offend or insult him. He is willing always to put his honor in jeopardy for them.

Clearly this parable departs from type as a tale of siblings. This father has two sons and there is no way they can escape from him.

Israel's Story

> [2] I have loved you, says the LORD. But you say, "How have you loved us?" Is not Esau Jacob's brother? says the LORD. Yet I have loved Jacob [3] but I have hated Esau; I have made his hill country a desolation and his heritage a desert for jackals.
>   MALACHI 1:2–3

A second way of understanding this parable draws on a variant of the sibling rivalry story. Israel has told her own story as a story of younger and elder brothers. The list is long and impressive.

- Cain and Abel
- Ishmael and Isaac
- Esau and Jacob
- Judah and his brothers versus Joseph and then Benjamin

The classic example is Esau and Jacob. Jacob steals Esau's birthright from his old, blind father with the connivance of his mother. Then he must flee the wrath of Esau. While in a foreign land tending his father-in-law Laban's sheep, he cheats Laban out of the better part of his flock. Jacob's inheritance explains in story how Israel is God's elect. Election is not a matter of something Israel has done, but a matter of being freely chosen, elected.

Malachi 1:2–3 is an example of this use of the elder and younger story. The opening of Malachi implies the story of Esau and Jacob, and like the king in the parable of the young son covered in dirt and the elder son scrubbed clean, God loves Jacob and hates Esau.

A much later rabbinic analysis of this theme makes evident how prevalent this theme is. The rabbis are commenting on Jeremiah 3:19, in which God addresses his people and describes how he will "give you a pleasant land, the most beautiful heritage of all the nations. And I thought you would call me, My Father, and would not turn from following me." In commenting on this passage, the rabbis draw on a parable about how a king loves better his younger son. This explains Israel's election, its being chosen freely by God.

Comment on Jeremiah 3:19

Can "heritage of all nations" mean anything except that the Land of Israel was desired and coveted by all the nations? Consider the parable of a king who was seated at his royal table. He had many children, but he loved the youngest one the most. He was about to apportion their inheritances. Among the parcels of land there was one of great beauty, which all the children coveted, and so the king said: 'Let this parcel of land remain as my own portion.' As Scripture says, 'The Most High apportioned to the nations their inheritance' (Deut. 32:8), but to whom did He finally give His own portion? To His youngest child, for the next verse says, 'The Lord's portion to His people, to Jacob the lot of His inheritance'

MIDRASH ON PSALMS 5.1

Not only is the two sons story directly implied in the parable's plot, but there are specific metonymic references to the cycle of patriarchal stories. When Jacob and Esau are reconciled, "Esau ran to meet him, and embraced him, and fell on his neck and kissed him, and they wept" (Genesis 33:4). These same terms are used of the father when he greets the younger son. Only it is not the elder brother (Esau) who is being reconciled to the younger son (Jacob), but the father. Yet the father is not meeting the younger son the way Esau met Jacob with a small army of four hundred men. Esau knows how male honor should be backed up. And in his greeting he kisses Jacob once, while the father kisses the younger son affectionately over and over.

When the younger son is welcomed back, one of the signs of his restitution is the father's "finest robe." When Rebekah plots with Jacob to usurp Esau's birthright, "Rebekah took the best garments of her elder son Esau, which were with her in the house, and put them on her younger son Jacob" (Genesis 27:15). These clear metonymic references to the Jacob/Esau story indicate what story is being retold here, and certainly the audience would puzzle out the clues. In this parable the father takes up the role of welcoming the rogue, again indicating the shame he is willing to bear to hold on to his sons.

Mother

This family is very small. In the parable we hear of younger and elder sons, a father, hired hands and slaves. But in the parable's economy and compression there are no other brothers and sisters and no mother.

I may be pushing the argument too far, but there are aspects of the father that suggest he is playing the mother's role. In the parable's first part the roles are very male — son, heirs; a father; division of property. All this suggests the world of males. But when the son begins to "come to his senses," he formulates his problem not as a lack of money, but a lack of bread. "Lots of my father's hired hands have more than enough to eat (literally, bread), while here I am dying of starvation!" This shift is important because it indicates in the parable a shift to female images. Cash is male; bread is female.

When we first see the father expectantly on the lookout for the son, he behaves in ways that are an affront to his male honor. He runs, he falls on the son's neck and kisses him over and over, like the woman anointing Jesus. The father behaves like a female, a mother, welcoming back her son.

Similarly when the father deals with the elder son, he abandons the expectations of male honor. He comes out to the son and entreats him. But more significantly, at the parable's conclusion, the father addresses the son with a term of endearment, "my dearest child." It is a mother's voice. Fathers in the ancient world were remote and distant from their sons. But this father behaves in ways that are typical of the mother, who had to maintain close ties with her sons as her only source of agency or influence. All this, of course, creates a complex and culturally ambivalent image of the father. Even more precarious is that this imaging of the father in the role of the mother challenges the fundamental male hierarchy as the model for understanding the sacred.

Act three

There is a missing third act in this parable. The conflict between the brothers is left unresolved. The younger brother is inside at his homecoming banquet, with all the trappings of being received back. Shoes on his feet, a signet ring of authority, and the finest robe. It would appear that he has been restored as the favorite or even that he has supplanted the elder brother. No doubt he thinks he is home free.

Meanwhile outside the elder brother is angry and upset, but with all the property and power. The parable gives no indication that the elder son goes in to the banquet. Actually the tense of the Greek verb indicates that the banquet is over. "We just had to celebrate and rejoice." The celebration is over.

So what happens next? The audience is perhaps asked to imagine a third act. Soon the father will die. Then what? If the sons continue on with their established scripts, they are headed for a collision. One will kill the other. Or they can follow the father's script and surrender their male honor and keep on welcoming, accepting, and being with the other.

They have a choice between being lost or found, dead or alive.

9

Shrewd Manager

Shrewd Manager

There was this rich man
  whose manager had been accused of squandering his master's property.
He called him in
  and said,
  "What's this I hear about you?
  Let's have an audit of your management,
    because your job is being terminated."
Then the manager said to himself,
  "What am I going to do?
  My master is firing me.
  I'm not able to dig ditches
  and I'm ashamed to beg.
  I've got it!
  I know what I'll do so doors will open for me when I'm removed from
  management."
So he called in each of his master's debtors.
  He said to the first,
  "How much do you owe my master?"
  He said,
  "A thousand gallons of olive oil."
And he said to him,
  "Here is your invoice;
  sit down right now
  and make it five hundred."
Then he said to another,
  "And how much do you owe?"
  He said,
  "A thousand bushels of wheat."
He says to him,

"Here is your invoice;
  make it eight hundred."
The master praised the dishonest manager because he had acted
shrewdly.
    LUKE 16:1–8

This is one of the strangest and most difficult of Jesus' parables. Two customary assumptions undermine most attempts to interpret the parable.

- The master is God.
- The economic system is capitalism.

Both of these assumptions are commonly, almost unconsciously made, and lead to the parable's misunderstanding. Those who believe that the master is God must find some way to make the master's commendation acceptable. How can he commend the unjust steward's behavior? A similar problem besets the interpretation of the Laborers in the Vineyard when the master pays all the laborers the same wage, those who have borne the heat of day, as well as those who have only worked an hour. Because we assume that the master is God, efforts are made to make the parable say something other than it does.

- We also unconsciously assume that the economic system implied in the parable is capitalism. This has several important consequences.
- We empathize with the master since we see him as being defrauded of his property.

Capitalist assumptions obscure the social structure implied by the parable.

Ancient struggles

The parable of the Shrewd Manager has proven difficult not just for modern interpreters but apparently from very early times. Concerning Luke 16:8b–13, an ancient appendage to the parable, C. H. Dodd famously observed, "We can almost see here notes for three separate sermons on the parable text" (p. 30). I'm not sure about the number three, but clearly the early Christians took a number of tracks in trying to "solve" the parable. The first effort involved adding the comment about the "children of this world" and the "children of light," a phrase and distinction used in the Qumran Dead Sea

Scrolls. This suggests it may be a very early addition to the parable. This first effort to understand the parable draws a contrast between the interpersonal dealings of worldly people and those of spiritual people. This set the pattern for subsequent interpretations.

The second set of interpretations carries on the comparative theme, shifting back and forth from earth to heaven, drawing an ever sharper distinction between the two until finally the question is posed whether a slave can be loyal to two masters. Now the parable becomes an example of how the world works, and by implication, how those attached to heaven do not.

Ancient Notes for a Sermon

1. "For the children of this world exhibit better sense in dealing with their own kind than do the children of light.

2. "I tell you, make use of your ill-gotten gain to make friends for yourselves, so that when the bottom falls out they are there to welcome you into eternal dwelling places. The one who can be trusted in trivial matters can also be trusted with large amounts; and the one who cheats in trivial matters will also cheat where large amounts are concerned. So if you couldn't be trusted with ill-gotten gain, who will trust you with real wealth? And if you can't be trusted with something that belongs to another, who will let you have property of your own? No servant can be a slave to two masters. No doubt that slave will either hate one and love the other, or be devoted to one and disdain the other. You can't be enslaved to both God and a bank account."

3. The Pharisees, who were moneygrubbers, heard all this and sneered at him. But he said to them, "You're the type who justify yourselves to others, but God reads your hearts: what people rank highest is detestable in God's estimation."

LUKE 16:8A–15

All of these additions to the parable remind me of the story of the preacher who wrote in the notes for his sermon, "Weak point. Pound hard on the pulpit!"

The final addition (3) is almost certainly that of the author of the Gospel of Luke since it ties this parable into the three parables of chapter 15. Chapter divisions did not come from the original authors, but were added much later. Versification did not come until the printing press, when both chapters and verses were standardized. The author of Luke's gospel sees this parable not as part of a separate chapter, but as part of the Travel narrative (Luke 9:51–19:27).

There are strong similarities between the parable of the Prodigals and the Shrewd Manager. Both begin in Greek with "There was a certain man." The same verb describes the actions of the younger son and the manager: they both squander what has been entrusted to them. Both face life-threatening situations. The younger son is near death from starvation, and the manager without the master's employment would soon face the same situation. The father's forgiveness is as unexpected as the master's commendation. Perhaps Luke is drawing a parallel between two cases of unexpected forgiveness and by so aligning the parable of the Shrewd Manager to the parable of the Prodigals, he turns it into the parable of the Foolish Master. He further establishes thematic unity with his own addition to the parable which calls attention to the Pharisees "who were moneygrubbers," and thus ties the parable back to the beginning of chapter 15 where the Pharisees were complaining that Jesus was eating with sinners. These four parables, the Lost Sheep, the Lost Coin, the Prodigals, and Foolish Master, are all arranged in Luke's gospel to justify Jesus' association with sinners, the unexpected forgiveness of God, and the rejection of the Pharisees.

While this may well be the way Luke attempts to understand this puzzling parable, it doesn't really work because it avoids the scandal so deeply felt in the parable. So we must turn our attention to the parable itself and see what clues it offers for its interpretation.

Modern struggles

A number of scholars have attempted to ferret out just what is happening in the parable. Because parables compress, leave out details, and we, not belonging to the original audience, do not share their understanding and assumptions, comprehending the situation can be difficult.

Let us begin with a few obvious observations.

- The situation describes men of wealth.
- The master is called "rich."
- The debts are very large.

> 1,000 gallons of olive oil
> 1,000 bushels of wheat
> • Both the manager and those in debt can read and write.

This clearly puts them in the elites and means we are not dealing with peasants. In cities maybe ten percent of the population was literate, while in rural areas two to three percent was the typical figure.

In Galilee at this time there was a strong push toward commercialization of farming. Small peasant farms were disappearing and being absorbed into large estates, which were overseen by managers. Peasants either were forced off the land or became indentured servants on the large estates. Frequently this consolidation of the land was accomplished through debt. In order to meet taxes and tolls peasants often had to borrow. If the harvest did not produce a large surplus, they were unable to pay off their debt and before long the farm was confiscated. The request to "forgive us our debts" in the Lord's prayer is not an idle spiritual request, but a peasant's plea of desperation.

How do we explain what the manager is doing? What are his responsibilities? Managers were frequently household slaves, highly trained and valued. This manager is not a slave because he is dismissed. So he is a retainer of the master. He carries out the master's business as his agent. He manages the property, takes out and makes loans, sells the farm produce. When he acts, it is the same as the master acting. He is expected to make the master a large profit and is allowed a little "honest graft" on the side to feather his own nest. The profit of fifty percent on the olive oil and twenty percent on the wheat seems about right. Since with olive oil risk of spoilage was greater, a greater profit was demanded. While these amounts seem excessive to us, they were normal in the ancient world. Thus the manager's account adjustments eliminated his master's profit.

The Accounting

The parable begins with a demand for an accounting. Once again we face a problem of translation. The Greek word translated by "was accused" is *diaballein* which means to slander, to lie about. The word *diabolic* comes from this same root. The devil is one who lies. Thus it could be better translated, "the manager was falsely accused." People have been spreading lies about the manager and now the rich man, his master, believes the lies. This may well explain why the manager does not protest the charges. He realizes the effort would be futile. He has been outsmarted in the constant warfare that goes on in an agonistic society. His enemies have bettered him.

The master demands an audit and dismisses the manager from his job.

The manager's situation is precarious. He is not simply out of work, as in a capitalist system. He can't just go to look for work somewhere else. He is homeless and without resources. He will soon be in a life or death situation, for he has no way to earn a living.

At this point the storyteller lets us in on the manager's interior monologue. This technique occurs in a number of Luke's parables and may represent his way of performing a Jesus parable. It's his embellishment of Jesus' parables, something we would expect from a talented writer like the author of the Gospel of Luke.

The manager envisions as his options two of the most disgraceful things in the ancient world. "To dig ditches" is too contemporary a reference. "To dig" in the Greek probably refers to digging in the mines which is slave work and nearly always a death sentence.

The quotation from Sirach makes clear that begging is also a condemnation to death. Someone who is reduced to begging is without resources. Without the patronage of his master, the manager is in real danger.

Begging

28 My child, do not lead the life of a beggar;
it is better to die than to beg.
29 When one looks to the table of another,
one's way of life cannot be considered a life.
One loses self-respect with another person's food,
but one who is intelligent and well instructed guards against that.
30 In the mouth of the shameless begging is sweet,
but it kindles a fire inside him.
Sirach 40:28–30

Digging and begging are images of his desperation.

He plots a course that will protect him. It's not exactly clear how he can get away with this proposal. Technically he is no longer the master's manager and so does not have the power to act as he is proposing. Obviously he plans to carry out his plot before the word has gotten around that he has lost his manager's position. Somehow he calculates he can get away with it.

Just what does the manager do to gain the good will of his master's debtors? Apparently he eliminates the profit or usurious interest. When the word gets back to the master of what has happened, he has two options.

- The master can repudiate his ex-manager's action. But this would involve severe loss of face on the master's part. When those whose debts have been so generously reduced begin to praise the master, it's unlikely he will risk owning up to what has happened.
- He can accept his ex-manager's action.

A Master's praise

"The master praised the dishonest manager because he had acted shrewdly."

The master's final comment not only takes the story in an unexpected direction, but it also makes it very difficult to make sense of the story. Every hearer or reader of the parable attempts to put it together in such a way that the conflicts or unresolved features of the story are resolved and fitted together.

At least three questions occur to us.

- Why is the master praising the manager? What does it mean for him to praise the manager?
- How can he praise him for being dishonest?
- How is the manager shrewd?

A warning is in order. As readers or hearers of the parable we strive to make sense of it, to fit it together. We can see from the three sets of additions to the parable that ancient readers also strove to make sense of the parable, to relieve the tension created by the story. But what if the strategy of the parable teller is to frustrate our efforts to fit it together, to make sense of it, to relieve its tension?

Dismissal?

The master had originally dismissed the manager because he had squandered the master's property. Now he commends him for acting shrewdly — the way a manager is supposed to act. If the master cannot repudiate the reductions in debt instituted by the manager without loss of face, do we have to imagine that the master let his dismissal stand or could he have taken the manager back? Is the master now convinced of the manager's shrewdness, even though what he did was dishonest? It could be argued that what we have here is a picture of the way masters and managers operate. In an agonistic culture, since the manager has done the master one better, perhaps the master has decided to keep him in his employ. After all, given the interest rates the master is expecting, a little dishonesty in his favor won't bother him at all.

The master himself is not so righteous. He has participated in and profited from his manager's efforts to charge exorbitant interest and make huge profits. It's not the manager's dishonesty that bothers the master, but his squandering of the master's property. Now that he has shown just how shrewd he is, why should the master not keep him in his employ?

Rogue

The manager plays the well-known role of a rogue who is getting even with the master for firing him. The rogue always engages in unlawful behavior, but he does so for a reason. Somehow he has been offended or cheated and he has to go outside the legal system to set things right. We enjoy the rogue's getting even because it allows us to go on a moral holiday. The rules are suspended.

In this parable the manager gets even with the master by appropriating the master's profit, which itself is morally suspect — for as we have seen no characters in this parable are innocent. When the master commends the manager for his shrewdness, he also reminds us that the manager is unjust or dishonest. We are reminded that the moral holiday is not really a holiday. Wrong has been done, lots of wrong on all sides.

Debts

The statement of the bill in terms of the amount of produce also calls for explanation. The Torah forbad interest, so ways around this prohibition inevitably developed.

Torah on Interest

[25] If you lend money to my people, to the poor among you, you shall not deal with them as a creditor; you shall not exact interest from them. [26] If you take your neighbor's cloak in pawn, you shall restore it before the sun goes down; [27] for it may be your neighbor's only clothing to use as cover; in what else shall that person sleep? And if your neighbor cries out to me, I will listen, for I am compassionate.
EXODUS 22:25–27

[35] If any of your kin fall into difficulty and become dependent on you, you shall support them; they shall live with you as though resident aliens. [36] Do not take interest in advance or otherwise make a profit from them, but fear your God; let them live with you. [37] You shall not lend them your money at interest taken in advance, or provide them food at a profit. [38] I am the LORD your God, who brought you out of the land of Egypt, to give you the land of Canaan, to be your God.
LEVITICUS 25:35–38

[19] You shall not charge interest on loans to another Israelite, interest on money, interest on provisions, interest on anything that is lent. [20] On loans to a foreigner you may charge interest, but on loans to another Israelite you may not charge interest, so that the LORD your God may bless you in all your undertakings in the land that you are about to enter and possess.
DEUTERONOMY 23:19–20

Since the laws forbidding interest are so clear, and since the development of commercial enterprises demanded taking interest, some accommodation had to be found. The way around this forbidding of interest was to state the interest in terms of commodity, as in this parable. Thus the Torah was circumvented.

In this parable the Torah, the will of God, is restored although that is the intention of neither the master nor the servant. The parable becomes a very clever example of how the elites carry on their business, while God's Torah gets accomplished in spite of their intentions.

Rich farmer

Surely Jesus is not holding up this kind of activity, dishonest on the part of both the master and the manager, as a way in which God's will is done. Yet another of Jesus' parables works in similar fashion.

Rich Farmer

There was a rich man whose fields produced a bumper crop.
"What do I do now?" he asked himself,
  "since I don't have any place to store my crops?
I know!"
he said,
  "I'll tear down my barns
  and build larger ones
      so I can store all my grain and my goods.
Then I'll say to myself,
  'You have plenty put away for years to come.
  Take it easy; eat, drink, and enjoy yourself.'"
But God said to him,
  "You fool!
  This very night your life will be demanded back from you.
  All this stuff you've collected — whose will it be now?"
      LUKE 12:16–20

This parable draws on the story of Joseph in Genesis 41. Joseph develops a strategy to solve an impending grain shortage in Egypt. After seven years of bountiful harvest there will be seven years of drought. The story reiterates over and over that Joseph *stores* up the surplus in *store*houses, so that when the drought comes, Egypt will have plenty of food. We all know how this story turns out. In the end Joseph's farsightedness allows him to save his own family, which had sold him into slavery, from starvation. Once again God acts through conduct that on the surface does not appear just. Out of the brothers' terrible action of selling Joseph into slavery came their salvation.

In this parable the farmer is blessed with a giant harvest and so he builds new barns to store up his fantastic bounty. But unlike Joseph

---

Joseph Stores up Grain

[47] During the seven plenteous years the earth produced abundantly. [48] He gathered up all the food of the seven years when there was plenty in the land of Egypt, and stored up food in the cities; he stored up in every city the food from the fields around it. [49] So Joseph stored up grain in such abundance — like the sand of the sea — that he stopped measuring it; it was beyond measure.

GENESIS 41:47–49

he is storing up the bountiful harvest not for the good of the people, but for his own selfish ends. This farmer is an epicurean. It is all stored up for his own good. "Take it easy, eat, drink, and enjoy yourself."

That night God demands his life of him. His plan to enjoy his stored up goods for his own ends is terminated. He dies a fool, one whose very activity has denied the existence of God. "The fool says in his heart, 'There is no God'" (Psalm 14:1).

God's purpose is fulfilled. The harvest will be available for the good of all. For bad years will inevitably come. In a limited goods society where there is only so much of everything to go around, a good harvest means a bad harvest is on the way.

In the future the villagers may well build a statue to honor the man who had the foresight to build such barns and store up the grain. After all, they do not know that God demanded the life of this fool. For them, he died in his sleep.

Both the parable of the Shrewd Manager and Rich Farmer tell compelling stories that on first hearing are quite scandalous and hard to fit together. Yet both make the point that God's will may well be accomplished in occurrences where it is hard to see God's action. It's very much like leaven.

10

Unforgiving Slave

Unforgiving Slave

A secular ruler decided to settle accounts with his slaves.
When the process began,
   this debtor was brought to him
      who owed ten million dollars.
   Since he couldn't pay it back,
      the ruler ordered him sold,
      along with his wife and children and everything he had,
      so he could recover his money.
At this prospect, the slave fell down
   and groveled before him:
   "Be patient with me,
   and I'll repay every cent."
Because he was compassionate,
   the master of that slave let him go
   and canceled the debt.
As soon as he got out,
   that same fellow collared one of his fellow slaves
      who owed him a hundred dollars,
   and grabbed him by the neck
   and demanded:
   "Pay back what you owe!"
His fellow slave fell down
   and begged him:
   "Be patient with me
   and I'll pay you back."
But he wasn't interested;
   instead, he went out
   and threw him in prison until he paid the debt.

When his fellow slaves realized what had happened,
   they were terribly distressed
   and went
   and reported to their master everything that had taken place.
At that point, his master summoned him:
   "You wicked slave,"
   he says to him,
"I canceled your entire debt because you begged me.
   Wasn't it only fair for you to treat your fellow slave with the same
      consideration as I treated you?"
   And the master was so angry
   he handed him over to those in charge of punishment
   til he paid back everything he owed.
    MATT 18:23–34

Only one of Jesus' parables is about a king, or secular ruler. Yet this theme is quite common in rabbinic parables, accounting for over half of them. While the empire of God is a principal theme in Jesus' teaching, he apparently doesn't prefer kings as models for his kingdom. Given the ruthlessness of the king in this parable and of kings in general, such reluctance is understandable. Jesus' view of God does not comport with imperial ambitions.

Better watch out

Matthew incorporated this parable into what is usually called his ecclesial discourse, his sermon about church order. This is the fourth of the five sermons that interrupt the narrative flow of Matthew's gospel. It is less a sermon than the others and more a question and answer period between Jesus and his disciples. But this "sermon" clearly belongs to the grouping of speeches because it has the formulaic ending that ends each sermon. "And so when Jesus had finished this instruction, he took leave of Galilee . . ." (Matt 19:1, see also 7:28; 11:1; 13:53; 26:1).

The instruction begins with Jesus' disciples asking, "Who is greatest in Heaven's domain?" As presented by Matthew, the disciples are clearly seduced by an imperial view of the church, while Jesus prefers the image of a child.

The instruction ends with the parable of the unforgiving slave, which Matthew situates as the answer to Peter's question, "Master, how many times can a companion wrong me and still expect my forgiveness? As many as seven times?" Jesus responds, "My advice to you is not seven times, but seventy-seven times." The answer employs a hyperbole to indicate an infinite number of times. The parable then illustrates this response of Jesus.

In order to link the parable as an illustration of Jesus' answer to Peter's question, Matthew has constructed an introduction for the parable: "This is why Heaven's imperial rule should be compared to . . ." The Greek phrase that begins that transitional opening, literally "therefore," frequently appears in Matthew to connect a Jesus saying to the context to make a point. "Should be compared to" is also a phrase that occurs only in Matthew (see 13:24 and 22:2).

Finally Matthew is also responsible for the conclusion drawn from the parable: "That's what my heavenly Father will do to you, unless you find it in your heart to forgive each one of your brothers and sisters."

To say the least, Matthew's use of the parable is very troubling. After Jesus demands of Peter almost infinite forgiveness, he then tells a parable in which the king after forgiving an almost unimaginable amount, turns around and punishes a slave after his first offense. So while Peter must forgive "seventy-seven times" the king is going to forgive only once. And since the king is a stand-in for God, this holds God to a much lower standard than Peter. Matthew's conclusion to the parable — that such is the way of God — drives home the point that God is really a very threatening character, hardly very merciful, more like an oriental tyrant. Since for Matthew the king is God, what are we to think of divine forgiveness if it is conditional, if it can be taken away? Only because Matthew has made the king God do readers not revolt against a king who demands multiple forgiveness but lashes out at the first failure.

Obviously Matthew is not much help in understanding the parable.

Three scenes

The parable has three scenes.

1. The king's accounting
2. The slave's accounting
3. The king's second accounting.

The first two scenes are structured in parallel but not identical fashion. In each scene the one owing a debt falls down and begs, "Be patient with me and I'll pay you back." Besides the parallel between the two scenes, there is a strong contrast.

- The debts are very different.
- The king has compassion and forgives, while the slave does not.

In between the middle scene and the final scene, the fellow slaves report to the king what has happened and their action provokes the final accounting.

Royal context

The situation pictured in this parable is that of a client king of the Roman emperor. It is not a particular client king, for instance one of the Herods, but any client king.

Several clues in the story indicate this. The use of king in the parable's first part points in this direction, although thereafter in the Greek he is called "master" or "lord." Some have taken this to mean that originally the parable did not involve a king but only a "master." But master or lord is a perfectly good title for a king and indicates the relationship between the characters.

The decisive piece of evidence that we are dealing with a king is the amount of money involved. It is almost unbelievable, an astronomical amount. Talent is the largest unit of money and 10,000 is the largest number. According to Josephus, the total yearly taxation for Judea during the Roman period was 600 talents and the tribute demanded from the Jews after Pompey's conquest of Judea was 10,000 talents, the amount mentioned in the parable.

A talent had originally referred to a weight, but at this period it designated a monetary unit equal to 6,000 denarii. If one denarius is a day laborer's wage, then to a Galilean peasant 10,000 talents is an unimaginable amount of money. I don't think we should take the amount as representing real money, but it is like what children do when they say "zillion billions." It's a fantastic amount.

It has been suggested that perhaps what is being recounted here is the taxation system of the Roman empire. A king would farm out the collection of taxes to the highest bidder, who would then hire other agents to do the actual collecting. At each transaction, a profit would be added, so that the final amount would far exceed the amount bid.

Taxation of Archaelaus' Dominions

When Caesar had heard these pleadings, he dissolved the assembly; but a few days afterwards he appointed Archelaus, not indeed to be king of the whole country, but ethnarch of the one half of that which had been subject to Herod, and promised to give him the royal dignity hereafter, if he governed his part virtuously. But as for the other half, he divided it into two parts, and gave it to two other of Herod's sons, to Philip and to Antipas, that Antipas who disputed with Archelaus for the whole kingdom. Now to him it was that Perea and Galilee paid their tribute, which amounted annually to **two hundred talents**, while Batanea, with Trachonitis, as well as Auranitis, with a certain part of what was called the House of Zenodorus, paid the tribute of **one hundred talents** to Philip; but Idumea, and Judea, and the country of Samaria paid tribute to Archelaus, but had now a fourth part of that tribute taken off by the order of Caesar, who decreed them that mitigation, because they did not join in this revolt with the rest of the multitude. There were also certain of the cities which paid tribute to Archelaus: Strato's Tower and Sebaste, with Joppa and Jerusalem; for as to Gaza, and Gadara, and Hippos, they were Grecian cities, which Caesar separated from his government, and added them to the province of Syria. Now the tribute-money that came to Archelaus every year from his own dominions amounted to **six hundred talents**.

JOSEPHUS, *Jewish Antiquites*, 17.11.4

This system may well be what lies behind the parable, and everyone hearing it would have been familiar with the system, if not the actual details.

Scene 1

Client kings were perched atop a hierarchical system which was built upon intrigue, power, and fear. A king had to scramble to get power and to maintain it. In his *Res Gestae* (see chapter 3) Augustus mentions numerous attempts by client-kings to seize power and how he dealt with them.

The various stories about Herod the Great and his successors reinforce this point. When Herod the Great (ruled 40–4 B.C.E.) was appointed King of the Jews, he first had to depose Antigonus II who still sat on the Judean throne. Caught up in the civil war between

Pompey Exacts Tribute from Jerusalem

Now the occasions of this misery which came upon Jerusalem were Hyrcanus and Aristobulus, by raising a sedition one against the other; for now we lost our liberty, and became subject to the Romans, and were deprived of that country which we had gained by our arms from the Syrians, and were compelled to restore it to the Syrians. Moreover, the Romans exacted of us, in a little time, above **ten thousand talents**; and the royal authority, which was a dignity formerly bestowed on those that were high priests, by the right of their family, became the property of private men.

JOSEPHUS, *Jewish Antiquites*, 14.4.5

Mark Antony and Octavian, he first sided with Antony, and after the battle of Actium (31 B.C.E.), he adroitly managed to switch sides. But all was not well within the family, and Herod was constantly involved in intrigues in order to stay in power. He imprisoned and executed many of his family members, including one of his wives and three of his sons. One of his sons, Herod Antipas, was tetrarch of Galilee and Perea (4 BCE to 39 CE). He too was involved in many intrigues, as the story of the death of John the Baptist makes evident. Antipas eventually fell victim to his own maneuvering. He went to Rome to protest his lack of royal status, was accused of crimes against Rome by the agents of his nephew and brother-in-law Herod Agripa, and was exiled to Gaul. Staying on top was not easy and demanded ruthless use of power.

To recapitulate, the amount of money owed is a fantastic amount, given the quotations above from Josephus, and since it is nearly impossible to conceive of an individual owing this amount, the suggestion that we are dealing with the tax farming system makes sense. Given the taxation burdens of Galilee, Jesus' audience would view this whole scene with a jaundiced eye.

When the imperial slave is unable to make the payment, the ruler orders him "sold, along with his wife and children and everything he had, so he could recover his money."

The philosopher Bion's story of the punishment his father received indicates the normalcy of such punishment. Kings had absolute power and they were accustomed to using it ruthlessly.

If the king throws the slave and his family into prison, how will he recover what is owed him? This is a patron-client society. The king is the chief patron and the slave is his client. This slave, because he is a powerful retainer of the king, is himself a patron for other clients and they in turn are patrons to yet other clients. In such a way the whole society is organized in a descending series of dependent relationships. The king's calculation is that the slave's clients will come to his rescue and make up what is lacking. After all, if their patron is in prison, they are without influence.

At the prospect of prison and losing all his influence, the slave falls down before his lord and master and in the Greek "worships him" or "does obeisance," which indicates the divine-like status of the king. He asks for patience, for time, on the king's part and promises to pay back everything he owes. Many commentators say that this request is impossible. A single individual could not possibly pay back so huge a debt. But if the situation is tax farming, we need not imagine that the slave needs to raise the whole amount, but only what remained to be raised of his bid. He is requesting sufficient time for him and his clients to raise what is missing from the required amount.

The narrator tells us that the king was compassionate, the same word used in the parable of the Samaritan to describe his action

Bion's Story

For, when Antigonus inquired: "Who among men, and whence, are you? What is your city and your parents?"

He [Bion], knowing that he had already been maligned to the king, replied, "My father was a freedman, who wiped his nose on his sleeve — meaning that he was a dealer in salt fish — a native of Borysthenes, with no face to show, but only the writing on his face, a token of his master's severity. My mother was such as a man like my father would marry, from a brothel. Afterwards my father, who had cheated the revenue in some way, was sold with all his family. And I, then a not ungraceful youngster, was bought by a certain rhetorician, who on his death left me all he had. And I burnt his books, scraped everything together, came to Athens and turned philosopher. This is the stock and this the blood from which I boast to have sprung.

"Such is my story."

DIOGENES LAERTIUS, *The Lives of Eminent Philosophers*, 4.46–47 (LOEB)

towards the man in the ditch. Just as that compassion was unexpected, so also is compassion on a part of a king. Kings are ruthless, not compassionate. Yet this king is so compassionate he forgives the whole debt! It's hard to say which is more remarkable — that the king is compassionate or that he forgave the whole debt. He has forgiven an enormous amount of money. In a limited goods society, the audience would wait for the other shoe to fall, as it does later in the parable.

These kinds of totally unexpected scenes are typical of parables. One thinks not only of the Samaritan's compassion, but also of the father's taking back without question the younger son, and the master's praise of his shrewd manager. But before we rush into a celebration of God's great forgiveness, we should pay more attention to the story's outcome.

Scene 2

When the slave goes out he meets a fellow slave who owes him one hundred denarii. This fellow slave is one of his clients, just as he is a client of the king. A debt of one hundred denarii is insignificant in comparison with ten thousand talents, but it is not insignificant in itself. If the average subsistence wage for a day laborer was one denarius a day, then this is equivalent to a hundred days' wages, a rather large sum for the Galilean peasants who made up Jesus' typical audience.

The slave's approach to his fellow slave betrays his character: he grabs him by the neck and demands, "Pay back what you owe!"

The fellow slave falls down before the slave-patron, just as the first slave fell down before his king-master. Perhaps "prostrate" would be a better translation in both cases. But this slave does not "grovel" or "worship" him, since that would be inappropriate. Instead he begs him with the same speech as the first slave had made to the king, but the slave-patron hardheartedly ships his client-debtor off to prison.

Scene 3

Between scene two and three the fellow slaves intervene. In their distress they report to the king everything that has happened. Thus their report precipitates the king's final action.

When the king summons the slave he calls him, "You wicked slave," thus signaling his change of disposition. Just as the first slave's action of grabbing by the throat signaled his character, so now the king's greeting signals his behavior.

The king raises the decisive question, "Wasn't it only fair for you to treat your fellow slave with the same consideration as I treated you?" This is the logic of the king's initial behavior. Like demands like. The failure to do like for like has provoked the fellow servants into reporting to the king. The king's response is extreme, as extreme and unexpected as his compassion and forgiveness were initially. The master turns the slave over to the torturers ("those in charge of punishment") until he has paid back everything. That is, they will kill him.

What has provoked this extreme reaction from the king? It's not just a matter of economics or justice. The slave has violated the king's honor and shamed him. He has violated the master's honor in a fundamental way. By not following his example, he has made a mockery of his forgiveness. By forgiving his client, the king intended to lessen the debts of his entire kingdom, but the slave has suspended the process at its very beginning. In order to protect his honor, the master will wipe out the shame this slave has brought upon him.

Messianic context

In trying to understand this parable in its first century Galilean Jewish context, it's important to remember the story that lies behind this parable. Fundamental to the notion of the messiah is that he is a king. "Anointed" denotes kingship, anointing makes one a king. Thus in the fantastic forgiveness of an immense debt, the king signals the fulfillment of jubilee hopes. But the slave's lack of forgiveness brings this jubilee hope to an end and the king's final action brings it crashing down.

The parable represents a fundamental challenge to popular notions of messianic kingship: the system of kingship has within it a fatal flaw. Because it is totally authoritarian, it is inherently unstable. The system of patron-client distribution of power demands that each member of the hierarchy constantly scramble for power, protecting what he has and trying to grab more. There is no way the system can distribute forgiveness or the blessing of jubilee.

A Trap

The parable contains a further trap. The parable's hearers who disapprove of the slave-patron's action towards his fellow slave are drawn into the same pattern of authoritarian power. The fellow slaves want the slave punished. So what do they do? They report him to the king and the king turns him over to the torturers. They and the audience who identifies with their complaint have done exactly the same thing that the first slave has done. Thus the parable catches everyone in evil, not intentional evil, but implicit, unanticipated, systemic evil. Even if the messiah came and initiated the jubilee of debt forgiveness,

---

Messiah

By the first century there was no fixed, technical meaning for messiah. The term means "anointed" and is generally applied to kings.

The Psalms of Solomon (70–45 B.C.E.) envisions a messiah who belongs to David's line, a human being possessed of special gifts of wisdom and righteousness. This reflects the Psalmist's opposition to the non-Davidic Hasmonean dynasty.

See, Lord, and raise up for them their king,
the son of David, to rule over your servant Israel
in the time known to you, O God.

He will gather a holy people
whom he will lead in righteousness;
and he will judge the tribes of the people
that have been made holy by the Lord their God.

There will be no unrighteousness among them in his day,
for all shall be holy,
and their king shall be the Lord Messiah.

PSALMS OF SOLOMON, 17:21, 26, 32 (The Old Testament Pseudepigrapha)

At Qumran there was expectation of two messiahs — a priestly messiah and a royal, Davidic messiah.

They shall depart from none of the counsels of the Law to walk in the stubbornness of their hearts, but shall be ruled by the primitive precepts in which the men of the Community were first instructed until there shall come the Prophet and the Messiahs of Aaron and Israel.
1QS 9.11 (VERMES)

Jubilee

Jubilee was the fiftieth year coming at the end of seven cycles of seven years each. In that year the land was to return to its original owners, all debts forgiven, and all slaves set free. Jubilee, named for the shophar (a trumpet made from a ram's horn), became a symbol of the messianic blessings. Leviticus 25 contains the biblical legislation for the practice.

[8]You shall count off seven weeks of years, seven times seven years, so that the period of seven weeks of years gives forty-nine years. [9]Then you shall have the trumpet sounded loud; on the tenth day of the seventh month — on the day of atonement — you shall have the trumpet sounded throughout all your land. [10]And you shall hallow the fiftieth year and you shall proclaim liberty throughout the land to all its inhabitants. It shall be a jubilee for you: you shall return, every one of you, to your property and every one of you to your family. [11]That fiftieth year shall be a jubilee for you: you shall not sow, or reap the aftergrowth, or harvest the unpruned vines. [12]For it is a jubilee; it shall be holy to you: you shall eat only what the field itself produces.

LEVITICUS 25:8–12

the imperial system of which the messiah is a part would not allow the process to go forward.

A wholly other system is needed, a system outside empire, outside honor and shame, outside patron-client, outside royal power.

The victors write history. As such it becomes the history of kings and queens, of princes and nobles, and often of popes. About most of humankind history is silent. This parable stands in condemnation of that view of reality. It points to the utter corruption and irredeemable character of a world organized by imperial rule.

The parable paints a bleak picture of every effort to organize the world on the model of the empire. Whatever the empire of God might be, it cannot be that.

11

Dínner Party

Dínner Party

Someone was giving a big dinner
  and invited many guests.
At the dinner hour the host sent his slave to tell the guests:
  "Come,
  it's ready now."
But one by one they all began to make excuses.
  The first said to him,
  "I just bought a farm,
  and I have to go
  and inspect it;
  please excuse me."
And another said,
  "I just bought five pairs of oxen,
  and I'm on my way to check them out;
  please excuse me."
And another said,
  "I just got married,
  and so I cannot attend."
So the slave came back
  and reported these (excuses) to his master.
Then the master of the house got angry
  and instructed his slave:
  "Quick!
  Go out into the streets and alleys of the town,
  and usher in the poor, and crippled, the blind, and the lame."
And the slave said,
  "Sir,
  your orders have been carried out,
  and there's still room."

And the master said to the slave,
   "Then go out into the roads and the country lanes,
   and force people to come in so my house will be filled.
Believe you (plural) me,
   not one of those who were given invitations will taste my dinner."
      Luke 14:16–24

A person was receiving guests.
   When he had prepared the dinner,
   he sent his slave to invite the guests.
The slave went to the first
   and said to that one,
   "My master invites you."
That one said,
   "Some merchants owe me money;
   they are coming to me tonight.
   I have to go
   and give them instructions.
   Please excuse me from dinner."
The slave went to another
   and said to that one,
   "My master has invited you."
That one said to the slave,
   "I have bought a house,
   and I have been called away for a day.
   I shall have no time."
The slave went to another
   and said to that one,
   "My master invites you."
That one said to the slave,
   "My friend is to be married,
   and I am to arrange the banquet.
   I shall not be able to come.
   Please excuse me from dinner."
The slave went to another
   and said to that one,
   "My master invites you."
That one said to the slave,
   "I have bought an estate,
   and I am going to collect the rent.
   I shall not be able to come.
   Please excuse me."
The slave returned
   and said to his master,
   "Those whom you invited to dinner have asked to be excused."
The master said to his slave,

"Go out on the streets
and bring back whomever you find to have dinner."
Buyers and merchants will not enter the places of my Father.
THOMAS 64

Three versions of this parable appear in the gospel traditions. The versions in the Gospels of Luke and Thomas
are very similar, while that in Matthew differs considerably.

The Wedding Feast

Heaven's imperial rule is like a secular ruler who gave a wedding
celebration for his son. Then he sent his slaves to summon those who
had been invited to the wedding, but they declined to attend.

He sent additional slaves with the instructions: "Tell those invited,
'Look, the feast is ready, the oxen and fat calves have been slaughtered,
and everything is set. Come to the wedding!'"

But they were unconcerned and went off, one to his own farm, one
to his business, while the rest seized his slaves, attacked and killed
them.

Now the king got angry and sent his armies to destroy those mur-
derers and burn their city. 'Then he tells his slaves: "The wedding celebration is ready but those we've invited didn't prove deserving. So go
to the city gates and invite anybody you find to the wedding."

Those slaves then went out into the streets and collected everybody
they could find, the good and bad alike. And the wedding hall was full
of guests.

The king came in to see the guests for himself and noticed this man
not properly attired. And he says to him, "Look pal, how'd you get in
here without dressing for the occasion?"

And he was speechless.

Then the king ordered his waiters: "Bind him hand and foot and
throw him where it is utterly dark. They'll weep and grind their teeth
out there. After all, many are called but few are chosen."
MATT 22:2–14

Matthew clearly has the same parable, but its deviations
have led to some debate as to whether Matthew has reworked
a Q parable similar to the one found in Luke, or has received
the parable already changed in his oral tradition. I incline
towards the former view. The themes of the parable are too
clearly Matthean not to be from the hand of the author of that
gospel.

In this case, the man giving a banquet is a king giving a wedding feast for his son. In the Matthean allegory those first invited are the Jews and when they reject the invitation to the wedding feast, the king destroys their city — clearly a reference to the destruction of Jerusalem. In the second invitation "the good and bad alike" is a clear reference to the church, which Matthew consistently views as mixed, as for example, in his interpretation of the parable of Wheat and Tares (Matt 13:37–43).

The guest without the wedding garment refers to those who do not produce proper fruit. The parable ends with the man being thrown out into the darkness where "they'll weep and grind their teeth," another favorite phrase of Matthew (Matt 8:12; 13:42, 50; 24:13; 24:51; 25:30).

In Matthew's hands the parable becomes an allegory of Jewish rejection, Christian acceptance, and final judgment.

Comparison of Luke and Thomas

In both the Gospels of Luke and Thomas the parable has two movements.

- Invitation to the wealthy
- Invitation to the others

But there are crucial differences: Thomas has reworked the excuses of those first invited, while Luke has modified the invitation to others.

Thomas's excuses

Unlike Luke who has three excuses, Thomas has four. We should immediately be suspicious of four excuses, since oral storytelling prefers threes. Furthermore the excuses given in Thomas all have to do with the management of business. Even the excuse dealing with a marriage, which finds a parallel in Luke, has to do with the management of the wedding feast. These excuses fit with Thomas's final warning, "Buyers and merchants will not enter the places of my Father."

Luke's addition and setting

Luke seems more concerned with those invited after the first reject the invitation. This fits with the way Luke's gospel situates the parable. The scene is set at the dinner of a prominent Pharisee (Luke 14:1) and the larger context is Luke's travel narrative (Luke 9:51–19:27). Jesus initiates a discussion of table manners, noting first that one should not initially go to the highest seat, but the lowest. Then the host will invite you to move up. In an honor/shame society, to be shamed by having miscalculated and assumed too honorable a place would be great loss of face. Jesus then turns this little bit of wisdom into a moral statement: "Those who promote themselves will be demoted, and those who demote themselves will be promoted" (Luke 14:11). From this he draws a bit of counter wisdom advising his host not to invite his friends or those whose presence would give him greater honor, but "Instead, when you throw a dinner party, invite the poor, the crippled, the lame, and the blind" (Luke 14:13). Then he says you will be truly congratulated! The parable is then related in Luke as an example of this counter wisdom.

In the parable when the master learns that all his invited guests have refused to come, he first tells his slave, "Quick! Go out into the streets and alleys of the town, and usher in the poor, and crippled, the blind, and the lame." This is, of course, the group Jesus has just advised the Pharisee to invite to his dinner. Most likely, the author of Luke's gospel is responsible for adding this note to the parable.

Just as Thomas added the repudiation of businessmen to the end of his version of the parable, so Luke added the rebuff to those who were originally invited to the banquet: they will never get another invitation. Those first invited in Luke's allegory are the Jews, and this conclusion fits with his rejection of the Jewish people.

All the authors have had their way with this parable, but its outline still shows through these adaptations. Luke has most likely preserved the first part of the parable intact, while Thomas is certainly closer to the master's response to the rejection of his invitation. Thus the original parable would have gone something like the following.

The Banquet
> A man was giving a big dinner
> and invited many guests.
> At the dinner hour the host sent his slave to tell the guests:

"Come,
  it's ready now."
But one by one they all began to make excuses.
  The first said to him,
  "I just bought a farm,
  and I have to go
  and inspect it;
  please excuse me."
And another said,
  "I just bought five pairs of oxen,
  and I'm on my way to check them out;
  please excuse me."
And another said,
  "I just got married,
  and so I cannot attend."
So the slave came back
  and reported these (excuses) to his master.
The master said to his slave,
  "Go out on the streets
  and bring back whomever you find to have dinner."

Invitation

Banquets of the rich followed a set form; they were not spur of the moment activities. One of their primary functions was to bring honor to a host. If honor is to be maintained, guests must show up. Thus part of the set form of a banquet was an invitation issued days before the banquet. Normally this invitation was delivered by a slave who either read it, if he were literate, or recited it. A number of papyrus invitations have survived.

Formal Invitation
Chaeremon invites you to dine at a banquet of the Lord Serapis in the Serapeum tomorrow, that is the 15th, from the 9th hour.*

After the formal invitation, a slave would return at the appropriate time to escort the guests to the banquet. At this point the parable begins.

*Serapis is an Egyptian God and Serapeum is a place of the God's worship.

Rejections

But something is wrong with this banquet. Every one of those who was invited has an excuse and refuses to come. It cannot be a coincidence that all those invited have excuses, every single one of them. The man is being snubbed. Instead of redounding to his honor, this banquet will create great shame.

Even the slightest attention to the excuses reveals their vacuity.

- Who would buy a farm before he inspects it?
- Who would buy five pairs of oxen, even a single ox, before checking it out?
- Who would accept an invitation to a banquet and forget that he was getting married on that day?

On their faces the excuses are without merit. Surely the man is getting the cold shoulder, and apparently by all his acquaintances.

Response

In Matthew's and Luke's versions of the parable, the master is angry. Since in Matthew he is a king, he destroys their city, again pointing out the brutal power of monarchy we saw in the parable of the Unforgiving Slave. In Thomas the master's anger is not reported. The note about anger is something that would likely be added in the telling of the tale, given the insult to the man's honor. With his honor so offended, he now must calculate how to respond. His options are not very good.

- He could cancel the banquet and sulk off. Not an adequate response.
- He could blacken the reputation of those who have dishonored him, but this risks backfiring because it calls attention to his own dishonor.

He orders his slave, "Go out on the streets and bring back whomever you find to have dinner." Perhaps he thinks that this will make those who have refused to come to the banquet jealous. He'll show them! But this is a weak response, and his former friends are more than likely just to laugh at him.

Whatever the man's strategy, the banquet he ends up with is very different from the one he planned. It is now a banquet of the dishonorable, and he is shamed.

Messianic banquet

The messianic banquet lurks around the edges of this parable in the same way as the great cedar of Lebanon insinuates itself into the parable of the Mustard Seed, or the story of the prophecy of the birth of Isaac echoes in the parable of the Leaven. These parables are not about these images, but the allusions are part of the resonance of the parables. These themes are part of the repertoire of teller and audience — a shared cultural world of references. Just as the idea of the messiah is not standardized in first century Judaism, so also the messianic banquet is not a well-defined idea. It is one way of imagining the end times.

Messianic Banquet

[9] And the angel said to me, "Write this: Blessed are those who are invited to the marriage supper of the Lamb."
REV 19:9

[6] On this mountain the LORD of hosts will make for all peoples a feast of rich food, a feast of well-aged wines,
of rich food filled with marrow, of well-aged wines strained clear.
ISAIAH 25:6

[37] Receive what the Lord has entrusted to you and be joyful, giving thanks to him who has called you to the celestial kingdoms. [38] Rise, stand erect and see the number of those who have been sealed at the feast of the Lord.
2 ESDRAS 2:37–41

The righteous and elect ones shall be saved on that day; and from thenceforth they shall never see the faces of the sinners and oppressors. The Lord of the Spirits will abide over them; they shall eat and rest and rise with that Son of Man forever and ever. The righteous and elect ones shall rise from the earth and shall cease being of downcast face. They shall wear the garments of glory.
1 ENOCH 62:13–15

The parable of the Banquet burlesques the messianic banquet just as the Mustard Seed burlesques the great cedar of Lebanon. The banquet proposed by the man might be a fitting model for the messianic banquet but the actual banquet is something else. It also points to the here and now as the place of the banquet, and to life on the streets among the peasants as the appropriate model for the banquet, not the world of the elites. Just as the parable of the Unforgiving Slave rejects the imperial model for the messiah, so this parable rejects the banquets of the elites as the model for the messianic banquet. God's banquet is something else.

12

Re-Imagining the World

After looking at a selection of Jesus' parables, we inevitably face the question of what they tell us about Jesus. In terms of writing a biography of Jesus, they furnish us almost nothing. But as a way of making sense of who Jesus was, they furnish the foundation. In parable Jesus re-imagined what he was about, an alternative way of living in the world.

To get at this question we must bring together what we have observed about the individual parables and focus them into a pattern to understand what Jesus was about. In what follows I have developed three different coordinates. I have borrowed my image from mathematics, where a coordinate is two or more numbers used to determine the position of a point. I have tried to develop these coordinates by seeing where the parables intersect with each other and other items from the Jesus tradition. Each coordinate is represented by a parable that provides the insight that allows me to sketch the general contour of the coordinate. I will expand the insight by relating various other sayings and deeds to form a coherent picture of each coordinate. If I have connected enough dots, then an image of Jesus' re-imagined world should appear. You can fill in the colors.

Coordinate One: The Leaven

In the voting of the Jesus Seminar, the parable of the Leaven attracted the highest ranking of any parable. I take that to be significant for two reasons.

• The parable has not figured strongly in anybody's reconstruction of the historical Jesus and has received little attention in the history of scholarship.

• The radical interpretation of this parable initiated by Robert Funk in *Jesus as Precursor* has won the day.

Here if anywhere the distinctive voice of Jesus can be heard.

Insight: God is unclean

The parable serves as vehicle for the empire of God. It arranges a series of words into a pattern that a hearer must decode. We can view the parable at two different levels. At the level of a sentence the parable appears to picture an everyday scene in which a woman mixes some leaven in dough to make bread. But even at the sentence level there are some oddities. The woman hides the leaven. She does not mix the leaven, as one might expect. Likewise, the Greek word used here is not the neutral Greek word for hiding, but a word with strong negative overtones: she conceals the leaven in the dough. Even more, the amount of dough is extraordinary. Three measures is about fifty pounds of flour, not the normal amount for a baking session; as such it produces a humorous image of the woman baking such a large amount. Surely she is baking for a party. So while at the level of a simple sentence the parable appears to be everyday, upon closer examination there are suggestions that things are not quite normal.

The second level at which to understand the parable is as a metaphor for the empire of God. At this level it produces a cacophony. Leaven is a symbol for moral evil, the unclean; unleaven is the proper symbol for the divine. At passover "For seven days no leaven shall be found in your houses; for if any one eats what is leavened, that person shall be cut off from the congregation of Israel" (Exodus 12:19). Twice Paul quotes the aphorism "A little leaven leavens the whole lump" (Gal 5:9; 1 Cor 5:6). The purpose of this aphorism is to warn that a little evil will corrupt everything. It parallels the American aphorism "One rotten apple spoils the whole barrel." And Jesus warns his disciples to "beware of the leaven of the Pharisees" (Mark 8:15). It is not too extreme to say that the juxtaposition of empire of God and leaven is blasphemous. The comparison of the Empire of Rome to leaven would be more appropriate. The empire of God is NOT like leavened, but UNleavened bread.

Besides this initial negative symbol, the parable piles on other problematic symbols: a woman hides or conceals until all is leavened. "Until it is all leavened" brings the process of corruption to completion. The only symbolically positive term in the parable is "three measures," which is most probably an allusion to the messianic banquet. When Abraham receives the three angelic messengers at the Oaks of Mamre, Sarah makes cakes from thee measures of flour (Genesis 18:6). The reference in the parable to three measures is where the parable at the sentence level bursts out of the everyday, because the amount is way beyond ordinary. It points to the extraordinary, a divine banquet.

This one sentence parable redefines the divine. The divine is identified with the unclean, the impure. The involvement of the divine with the unclean does not result in the unclean becoming clean. The parable does not end with "until it was all *un*leavened." That would be a real miracle. Thus the divine becomes unclean, or to restate this insight even more provocatively: God becomes unclean. This is the fundamental insight on which I will build an understanding of what Jesus was about, of how he re-imagined the world.

Convergence: snakes and doves

Literally the parable makes no sense. God by definition cannot be unclean, and this is why the tradition has resisted the normal meaning of leaven and instead has sought to understand the parable in a non-threatening, actually reassuring way — from a little beginning comes a great end. So radical is the proposition that God is unclean, so counter-intuitive to normal religious thinking, indeed so offensive, that in order to demonstrate its correctness I must show how it makes sense of items in the Jesus tradition, how it can serve as a unifying insight into how Jesus re-imagined the world.

In this section I want to show how this initial insight converges with other items from the sayings and deeds of Jesus that the Jesus Seminar voted Red or Pink. This allows further expansion of the insight as well as producing what I hope is a convincing pattern within this database. The pattern or arrangement should begin to make sense of the isolated sayings and deeds.

The insight that God becomes unclean goes a long way toward explaining the frequent references to Jesus' association with the outcast, lepers, and sinners as well as the special place of women in his activity. These people find themselves accepted as they are without the need to become clean or honorable. The Congratulations also belong to this coordinate, for they congratulate people who are not obviously to be congratulated. The poor are congratulated because they are poor and to them belongs the empire of God, not because they will be rich. The Woe to the Rich, which Luke or Q probably added, simply draws the logical conclusion from the Congratulations to the Poor. This overturns the assumption that underlies the books from Deuteronomy to 2 Kings, namely that poverty and disease are God's punishment for sins.

"What goes in" is an explicit application of this insight to food laws. The argument that it is not what goes into the mouth that defiles

---

God is Unclean

Able-bodied and sick
Matt 9:12, Mark 2:17
Luke 5:31

Assassin
Thom 98:1–3

Congratulations: hungry
Luke 6:21, Matt 5:6.
Thom 69:2

Congratulations: poor
Luke 6:20. Thom 54, Matt 5:3

Congratulations: sad
Luke 6:21, Matt 5:4

Corrupt judge
Luke 18:2–5

Eye of a needle
Matt 19:24, Luke 18:25,
Mark 10:25

Foxes have dens
Luke 9:58, Matt 8:20,
Thom 86:1–2

Leaven
Luke 13:20–21, Matt 13:33.
Thom 96:1–2

Mustard seed
Thom 20:2–4, Mark 4:30–32,
Luke 13:18–19, Matt 13:31–32

No respect at home
Thom 31:1. Luke 4:24,
John 4:44, Mat 13:57,
Mark 6:4

Scholars' privileges
Luke 20:46, Mark 12:38–39,
Matt 23:5–7, Luke 11:43

Shrewd manager
Luke 16:1–8

Sly as a snake
Matt 10:16. Thom 39:3

Toll collector and Pharisee
Luke 18:10-14

Treasure
Matt 13:44, Thom 109:1–3

Two friends at midnight
Luke 11:5–8

What goes in
Mark 7:14–15, Thom 14:5,
Matt 15:10-11

a person, but what comes out, upsets the ability of the food laws to define what is clean and holy. Jesus appears to have carried out this aphorism literally in his eating habits by not washing his hands and by eating with unclean people. The function of food laws is to codify the divine so one can know where the divine is. But if foods can no longer represent and replicate the divine by marking the line between clean and unclean, then people can no longer be divided into clean and unclean.

This same rejection of the line between the clean and unclean finds expression in several parables. The planting of Mustard Seed, a weed-like plant, pollutes the garden, makes it unclean. Various revisions of the parable have obscured this aspect, though it is clear in Q's (Luke) version. Likewise, the Treasure, a gift, becomes a seduction for the man who, in his joy at finding the treasure, rushes out to do an immoral thing. He buries the treasure and goes and buys the field, thus signaling that the treasure is not his. He steals it from its rightful owner. This parable is a counterpoint to the Leaven. What is good, a treasure, seduces the man into doing evil.

Belonging to this same coordinate is the Eye of a Needle. The rich man is like treasure, one who according to Deuteronomy should be congratulated, but it will be more difficult for him to enter the empire of God than for a camel to pass through the eye of a needle.

Likewise the warning against the Privileges of Scholars, "who like to parade around in long robes," belongs here. Scholars know what is clean and unclean and who can thus represent the divine. But they should not be imitated, for the basis on which their scholarship rests has been undermined. The complex of sayings dealing with the Able-bodied and Sick clearly indicate that God is on the side of the sick. It is they who need a physician. God identifies not with the honorable and righteous, but the shamed and sinners.

Finally, into this coordinate I would place those parables which exhibit characters who do not quite seem to conform to the standard of behavior generally thought appropriate to the empire of God. For example, a hearer is shocked by the violence of the Assassin who tests his power by thrusting his sword through a wall. Like the deceit of the man who finds Treasure, the wheeling and dealing of the Shrewd Manager has confounded various interpreters since before the parable was incorporated into the gospel tradition. When dismissed from his job as manager, he goes to those who owe a debt to his master and drastically reduces their debt. But the manager's master is no saint either. He has long been profiting from the manager's shrewdness and usurious rates of interest.

The shamelessness of the man who delays in welcoming his guest in Two Friends at Midnight and the Corrupt Judge who fears neither God nor people in dealing with the widow's request both exhibit behavior that confounds an audience. The very amorality of the parables has proven problematic for most interpreters, to the point that the tradition has tried to explain it away. In the end, it is not the Pharisee who openly gives God thanks, but the Toll Collector standing at the back of the temple begging for mercy who goes home acquitted. The temple no longer sets the rules.

"No prophet is welcome on his home turf" because there the rules are known, and one who questions the rules is homeless. Unlike the Foxes Who Have Dens, the son of Adam has no place to lay his head. Jesus' probable conflict with his family and village belongs to this coordinate.

What is one to do in a situation where leaven represents the empire of God, when what goes into a person does not defile, where toll collectors go home acquitted, the poor are congratulated and home has disappeared? "You must be as sly as a snake and as simple as a dove."

Coordinate Two: Empty Jar

In contrast with the Leaven, the parable of the Empty Jar barely made the list of authentic sayings of Jesus compiled by the Jesus Seminar. There are a number of reasons for this.

- The parable occurs only in Thomas.
- There is little history of scholarship concerning this parable.

While these two reasons alone make me hesitant to build a significant coordinate on this parable, it does unambiguously illustrate the paradox of this coordinate.

Insight: God is present in absence

At the most elementary discourse level, the parable of the Empty Jar is about loss. The woman starts out with a jar full of grain but arrives home empty-handed. "The handle of the jar broke . . . She didn't know it . . . she put the jar down and discovered that it was empty." The empire is identified with loss, with accident, with emptiness.

It is possible that the story of Elijah's miracle for the widow of Zarephath as told in 1 Kings 17:8–16 lies in the background, furnishing a contrast story to the parable. During a famine, a widow feeds Elijah. When he first approaches her she says, "I have nothing baked, only a handful of meal in a jar, and a little oil in a jug." Elijah commands her to bake, but to bring him the first cake. "For thus says the Lord the God of Israel, 'The jar of meal shall not be emptied . . . until the day that the Lord sends rain upon the earth.'" She does as Elijah commands, and the prophet, she, and her child have meal and oil throughout the famine. The parable of the Empty Jar presents a contrast to the story of the widow with a full jar. There is no prophet to come to her aid, no end-time miracle to set things right.

Even if I am not correct about the Elijah counter reference, the basic narrative is clear. There is no divine intervention, she goes home empty-handed. This leads me to my second foundational insight: the empire of God is identified not with divine intervention but divine absence. Recasting the insight will help to bring it into focus: God is not found in the apocalyptic miracle — one must look elsewhere.

This parable brings out aspects of the profile which were only intimated in the Leaven. Like the Leaven it identifies the empire of God with the marginalized, the female, the unclean: and in the end if all is leavened, the jar is empty.

Convergence: Spread out but not seen

The saying that most obviously belongs to this coordinate is the Coming of God's Imperial Rule. This saying explicitly rejects the ability of people to point to or observe the empire of God. "On the contrary, God's imperial rule is right there in your presence." Both the Thomas and Lukan versions of the saying agree on these two basic points:

- you cannot point to it,
- yet it is here.

This presence of the empire of God, not able to be observed but in your presence, spread out upon the earth but not seen, indicates the paradox that the empire of God is present in absence. There is divine action occuring in the empire of God, but it cannot be observed.

The first Congratulations help us understand this coordinate of sayings. It says "Congratulations, you poor! God's domain belongs to you." They are in the empire of God and are still poor. It does not say,

Present in Absence

Anxieties: birds
Luke 12:24. Matt 6:26

Anxieties: don't fret
Thom 36:1, Luke 12:22–23,
Matt 6:25

Anxieties: clothing
Matt 6:28

Anxieties: lilies
Luke 12:27–28, Matt 6:28-30,
Thom 36:2

Anxieties: one hour
Luke 12:25, Matt 6:27

Congratulations: poor
Luke 6:20, Thom 54, Matt
5:3

Corrupt judge
Luke 18:2–5

Empty jar
Thom 97:1–4

Finger of God
Luke 11:19–20, Matt
12:27–28

God's imperial rule
Thom 113:2-4, Luke 17:20-21

Lost sheep
Luke 15:4–6, Matt 18:12–13

Mustard seed
Thom 20:2–4, Mark 4:30-32,
Luke 13:18–19, Matt 13:31–
32

Rich farmer
Thom 63:1–8, Luke 12:16-20

Satan divided
Luke 11:17–18, Matt 12:25-
26

Satan's fall
Luke 10:18

Seed and harvest
Mark 4:26–29

Sower
Mark 4:3–8, Matt 13:3-8,
Thom 9:1–5, Luke 8:5–8

Unforgiving slave
Matt 18:23-34

"Congratulations, you poor, for you shall be rich or at least middle class." The activity of God will not be manifested in a change from poor to rich. It is manifest in the paradox that to the poor belongs the empire of God. To say that God is present in absence is the same as saying that to the poor belongs the empire of God.

In the Mustard Seed the plant does not become the great cedar of Lebanon, the more appropriate metaphor for an empire. The mustard plant is more like a weed. In the Seed and Harvest, the harvest belongs to a farmer who does not quite know what is going on. He does not observe the activity of God because he is asleep. But the last line of the parable echoes a passage in Joel about the end-time, a scene of apocalyptic war. "Prepare war, . . . Beat your plowshares into swords and your pruning forks into spears; . . .Put in the sickle, for the harvest is ripe" (Joel 3:9-13). However, when the farmer puts in his sickle the occasion is not the ultimate end-time war between nations, but simply the actions of a farmer who is bringing in the harvest. And even though the parable of the Sower moves towards the expectation of a dramatic harvest as a climax to its stages of failure, the harvest is quite ordinary. It is not a harvest in which one grape makes five and twenty measures of wine, as in the Rabbinic speculations on the great harvest.

If images of apocalyptic expectation are rejected, the observer will need to be very acute and wary. Instead of protecting the ninety-nine, the shepherd may abandon the whole flock for the one that wandered away (Lost Sheep). Not a very good bargain. And the judge who does not fear God may be the one to vindicate the widow (Corrupt Judge). To push the case even further, it may be dangerous to ask for God's intervention. In the parable of the Unforgiving Slave, after the king forgives the slave's astronomical debt, his fellow slaves observe his lack of forgiveness of another slave — who by comparison owes a very small amount — and report it to the king who thereupon recants his forgiveness of the debt and turns the man over to the torturers. This king is a real Hellenistic autocrat. By turning in the first slave in the name of a greater justice the fellow slaves have done the same thing to him that he had done to the slave who owed him a debt. And now the king has made the situation even worse. Now they are dealing with a real tyrant. They have no criteria for his behavior. He may forgive everything or take it all back. The imperial order is no model for God's empire.

What is one to do in such a situation? One has to be very observant and see what is actually there. "Grapes are not harvested from thorn trees, nor are figs gathered from thistles" (from the complex On Anxieties: Don't Fret). Whole complexes of various sayings that deal with anxiety fit in here (On Anxieties: Don't Fret, Lilies, Birds, Clothing, One Hour). One should not worry about clothes or eating or anything else.

The parable of the Rich Farmer tells the other side of this story. Having a bounteous harvest, he tears down his barns and builds new ones. Yet that night he dies. His anxiety did him no good. Both the parables of the Empty Jar and the Rich Farmer move from bounty (full jar, great harvest) to loss (empty jar, death). God is not to be found in the apocalyptic vision.

Several recent studies of Jesus have put the healing and exorcisms of Jesus at the heart of their reconstruction. Even though it is difficult to trace individual stories of healing and exorcisms back to the earliest levels of the Jesus tradition, there can be no doubt that Jesus was a healer and exorcist. How does that activity of Jesus fit into this coordinate that I am developing? Does it not seem to contradict it?

The most explicit saying in which Jesus refers to his exorcisms attributes what he does to the finger of God. "If by God's finger I drive out demons, then for you God's imperial rule has arrived." In Moses' contest with the magicians of Pharaoh's court, when Aaron strikes the dust, a great swarm of gnats appears. Unable to duplicate the feat, the magicians tell Pharaoh, "This is the finger of God" (Exodus 8:15). Using this allusion to compare Jesus' exorcisms to Moses' wonderworking is like calling a Mustard Plant a tree and invoking the image of the great cedar of Lebanon. Both make an ironical claim that burlesques expectations.

In a similar vein, the saying about Satan's house being divided against itself (Satan Divided) indicates that there were those who saw Jesus' activity as that of Satan himself. Thus the power behind Jesus' exorcisms is not obviously God's, but can be mistaken for Satan's. If leaven is the model, no wonder such a mistake is possible. Perhaps this is the context in which one should view Jesus' claim to have seen Satan Falling from Heaven like lightning. Jesus views healings and exorcisms as divine activities, but they are not the overwhelming miracles of Moses, nor does his wonder working fill up the empty jar. It still demands insight on the part of the audience. He begins by saying, "IF by the finger of God," indicating that the viewer must judge what kind of activity this is. And some will judge it to be the activity of Satan.

Coordinate three: The Samaritan

The Samaritan received a very high vote of confidence from the Jesus Seminar even though the gospel of Luke contains the only surviving version. This parable is one of the most popular in the tradition and one of the most frequent topics in religious art.

Insight: Cooperation, not contest

To understand this narrative parable we must take up the point of view of a Jewish audience, and thus firmly set aside the gentile perspective in which the Samaritan is a good fellow, as Luke and the tradition have insisted. From the perspective of a first century Palestinian audience, the Samaritan is the expected opponent or villain, the moral equivalent of Leaven, and assigning the hero's role to him — instead of the priest or Levite or even the expected Israelite — is the same as finding the jar empty.

Even more, this parable envisions interpersonal relations existing on a basis other than an eternal contest. In a Mediterranean culture relations of all types were agonistic, i.e. viewed as a contest, because all goods were viewed as limited to a fixed amount and so one is always be in a competition, an agon, to get one's share of what is limited. To accept this parable as anything but a fantasy, a hearer must accept the Samaritan as helper-hero instead of expected opponent-villain, and visualize oneself as the victim in the ditch. An audience is not even offered the opportunity of an agonistic contest in the narrative. The man is passive in the ditch and the Samaritan acts out of compassion, effectively ending the story in mid-narrative. The Samaritan cannot even be the man's patron because their social spaces are so different. This leads to my third fundamental insight: The parable re-imagines human relationships apart from an agonistic social environment. Cooperation, not competition, is the basis for human social structure in the empire of God.

Convergence: The great leveling

Jesus' meals are probably the immediate context in which this coordinate found its most concrete expression. Eating together, sharing food in a society constantly threatened by hunger and famine, concretely demonstrated what cooperation meant. This is the context in which I would seek to understand the second and third Congratulations, which deal with hunger and weeping. The archetype is "Congratulations, you poor." In that beatitude there is no future in which the poor become rich. That beatitude should guide our understanding of the other two. "You will have a feast" and "You will laugh" do not refer to the apocalyptic future, but to the practice of cooperation within the meal events. There all will share what they have. So profound is this cooperation, so deep does it reach into the established structures of first-century reality, that the Samaritan can be envisioned as the hero-helper, and people can be commanded to "Love your Enemies."

The other side of this occurs in the Rich Farmer. He identifies him-

Cooperation not contest

Bury the dead
Matt 8:22, Luke 9:59–60

Children in God's domain
Mark 10:14, Matt 19:14,
Luke 18:16

Coat and shirt
Matt 5:40, Luke 6:29

Congratulations: hungry
Luke 6:21, Matt 5:6,
Thom 69:2

Congratulations: sad
Luke 6:21, Matt 5:4

Dinner party
Thom 64:1–11,
Luke 14:16-23

Emperor and God
Thom 100:2, Mark 12:17,
Luke 20:25, Matt 22:21

Foxes have dens
Luke 9:58, Matt 8:20,
Thom 86:1–2

Give to beggars
Matt 5:42, Luke 6:30

God as father
Luke 11:2, Matt 6:9

Hating one's family
Luke 14:26

Leased vineyard
Thom 65:1–7

Left and right hands
Matt 6:3. Thom 62:2

Lend without return
Thom 95:1–2, Matt 5:42

Love your enemies
Luke 6:27, Matt 5:44, Luke
6:32, 35

Lord's prayer: debts
Matt 6:12

On anxiety: Clothing
Matt 6:28a

Other cheek
Matt 5:39, Luke 6:29

Prodigal sons
Luke 15:11–32

Rich farmer
Thom 63:1–6, Luke 12:16-20

Samaritan
Luke 10:30–35

Saving one's life
Luke 17:33

Second mile
Matt 5:41

Shrewd Manager
Luke 16:1-8a

True relatives
Matt 12:46–50, Thom 99:2,
Luke 8:21

Two masters
Luke 16:13. Matt 6:24,
Thom 47:2

Unforgiving slave
Matt 18:23–34

Vineyard laborers
Matt 20:1–15

self as an epicurean: "Then I'll say to myself, 'You have plenty put away for years to come. Take it easy, eat, drink, enjoy yourself.'" He reserves a fantastic harvest for himself. But that night he dies, and so his harvest, like Joseph's in Egypt, will be available for the village. God does intervene in this parable, but to the villagers who helped the rich man build new barns, his death will be a natural one. Perhaps they will mourn for this "generous" man who has provided for them, but they will not see the hand of God in his death, because without his death, they would have starved. But intervention there was, for he intended to keep the whole harvest for himself.

The saying about Children in God's Domain indicates who people the empire of God. Children are an appropriate image because they cannot play the adult roles which are being rejected as inappropriate for life in the empire. In a patron-client society with the emperor at the top, a child is the most contrary image imaginable. The recasting of the family is fundamental to this redefinition of community. True Relatives are no longer one's natural family, but "Those here who do what my Father wants are my brothers and my mother." The other side of this redefinition is the veritable Hating of One's Family, extending even to the abandonment of a fundamental familial duty to bury the dead: "Leave it to the dead to bury their own dead."

This re-envisioned family contains a re-imagining of God as Father. The Seminar voted overwhelmingly that Jesus used "Abba" to refer to God as father. Regardless of how Abba is to be understood, clearly the tenor of "father" as a metaphor for God is very different from that in "Our Father in heaven." The latter is part of the patriarchal, patron-client world; the former is an effort to redefine family.

The parable of the Prodigal Sons exhibits in great detail a narrative of this re-imagined family. The father in the parable at times plays a foolish and shameless role and at other times a "female" role. From the very beginning of the narrative he exhibits little in the way of male honor. The admonition of Sirach about the distribution of inheritance is clear. "While you are still alive and have breath in you, do not let any one take your place. It is better that your children should ask from you than that you should look to the hands of your sons. . . At the time when you end the days of your life, in the hour of death, distribute your inheritance" (Sirach 33:21-23). The father of this parable surrenders his property, putting himself and his family at risk. He runs and kisses his younger son instead of maintaining his male dignity, and he addresses the elder son as "my dear child."

Even more, the father does not choose between his sons. He

accepts both regardless of what they do. The acceptance of one is not purchased at the cost of the rejection of the other, as is typical of such stories of elder and younger sons in the Hebrew Bible and other cultures.

Finally, there is a third act implied but unspoken in the narrative. The story ends with a younger son, feasting on the fatted calf with all the signs of acceptance — shoes on his feet, a signet ring on his finger and the father's best robe as his garment — thinking he has struck a clever bargain with the father. Meanwhile, outside waits an angry elder son who still has all the property. What happens when the father dies? If the sons continue on their same trajectories, the younger pushing the boundaries, the elder feeling himself the abused family slave, someone is going to be killed. Or they can emulate the father. He is all acceptance. There is nothing the sons can do that he will not accept, regardless of the cost to him. He is willing to surrender all his male honor to preserve his sons in family. Or as another saying has it, "Whoever tries to hang on to life will forfeit it, but whoever forfeits it will preserve it" (Saving One's Life).

While exactly what is at stake in the Leased Vineyard is not very clear, it surely represents an agonistic struggle run amuck. The owner who relies on the respect due him as a patron and social superior misjudges the intent of those who have leased his vineyard. These also calculate that they can get away with their acts of violence. The parable exhibits how bankrupt is a world based on competitive strife. It is a world of unending violence.

In the Vineyard Laborers, the first hired complain that by paying the last hired the same amount they have received, the master has made them equal. Their essential complaint is that the master has destroyed the order of the world. The entire Roman empire was organized as a patron-client system. The ultimate patron was the emperor, and power worked its way downward, with his clients in turn becoming patrons for yet other clients. And their fleas have fleas, too. Such a system ensures a hierarchically arranged social order in which no one is equal and every social engagement is a contest to determine one's place in the hierarchy.

The one issue for which Jesus appears to have a program is indebtedness. The Lord's Prayer explicitly calls for the forgiveness of debts and Jesus advises to Lend without Return. In a society where peasants were crushed by debt and were being displaced from their land, this is no idle wish, but a concrete program to rebuild community. The empire of God is clearly part and parcel of this rebuilding. The parable of the Shrewd Manager pictures the forgiving of debt, even when not intended by the elites, and the parable of the Unforgiving Slave warns that the imperial model can bring neither the messiah nor the jubilee.

If one were to take seriously the debt question and its corollary Give to Beggars, then one would have no Anxieties about Clothing and one would probably be homeless. Unlike the Foxes who have Dens, the Son of Adam has no place to lay his head.

Visualizing the empire of God as family puts everyone on the same level. The effect of this leveling is seen from the rich man's point of view in the Dinner Party. In order to throw his party, he must invite the homeless and forfeit the company of those rich like himself. So radical is the disconnect between these two ways of organizing social relations that one cannot have Two Masters, something demanded by the patron-client organization of society. Calculating which master to please is a hazard of everyday life. The organization of the emperor's world is diametrically opposed to that of God's. "Give the emperor what belongs to the emperor, give God what belongs to God."

This re-imaging of social relations finds one of its clearest expressions in those sayings burlesquing case law: Other cheek, Coat and Shirt, Second Mile, Give to Beggars, Lend without Return. The purpose of case law is to work out in advance and in detail all the situations or cases implied by a law. These sayings of Jesus burlesque case law through a similar form and strategy. If someone asks for your shirt, give them also your coat. In such a case one would soon be naked. If you turn the other cheek, you would soon be black and blue, beaten about the face. And finally if you gave every time someone begged, you would soon be broke. These lampoons of case law subvert the very effort of case law to specify what is moral. "When you give charity, don't let your left hand know what your right hand is doing."

Outcomes

The world implied in these three coordinates re-imagines a community's social experience. The empire of God as Leaven does not warrant a license to do whatever one wants. Rather, the unclean are accepted as welcomed by God just as they are without the necessity of becoming clean. Likewise when the empire of God is an empty jar, then the community must accept responsibility for its own welfare and not fall back on the narcotic of a divine intervention to set things right. When the Samaritan is the hero-helper, then social cooperation is defined outside the bounds of the traditional agonistic dynamic of a patron-client relationship. These three aspects go a long way towards redefining basic human relationships as conceived within a Mediterranean peasant culture.

Death of Jesus

The reason(s) for the death of Jesus probably remain beyond our grasp. Empires can and do act in arbitrary and authoritarian ways that escape the cool rationality of law or reason. Pilate did not really need a solid case to kill Jesus. Yet one can see in Jesus' language-activity the seeds of a conflict that could easily escalate to a confrontation and to death. And the parable of the Leaven and what it implies are sufficient blasphemy to have put Jesus into conflict with the religious authorities. For them the symbol of God's activity is unleavened bread, the clean. The leavened bread must be swept out to make a place pure and holy, set apart. And even though Jesus explicitly separates God's empire and Caesar's, the success of Jesus' social experiment in peasant community under the symbol of the empire of God would pose a threat to Rome's rule. For Empire is built on the premise that the local populations are divided and distrustful of each other. A peasantry who accept each other, who no longer see themselves in agonistic conflict with each other, no longer defending their given and limited positions but even reaching out to Samaritan enemies — such a peasantry poses a real threat to Rome's rule by thwarting its attempts to divide and conquer.

Empire as symbol

The empire of God is at the core of Jesus' re-imagining. It is the presiding symbol, whether or not it is always or ever the referent of the parables. Also the understanding of the empire of God must be derived from Jesus' language-activity, rather than from an historical survey of Jewish literature. Such a survey produces little fruit because of the very infrequent appearance of the phrase. Empire of God is a symbol standing for the experience that results from participation in the language-activity of Jesus. The Coming of God's Imperial Rule clearly indicates that it is a non-empirical reality. "You won't be able to observe the coming of God's imperial rule. People are not going to be able to say, 'Look, here it is!' or 'Over there.'"

Jesus surely uses empire in an ironical sense, since the empire of God fails to measure up when compared to the empires of David or Caesar. The irony of this failed comparison is clearly represented in the Emperor and God: "Give the emperor what belongs to the emperor, give God what belongs to God." To define it negatively, the empire of God is not like the empire of David or Caesar. As a symbol, the empire of God is like the American flag. It stands for a whole series of complex values which cannot be expressed clearly — that is why one needs to employ a symbol to represent it. But to go even further, I think the empire of God functions to create through the imagination a sphere in which those who are a part of this community of envisioning and re-imagining can experience healing, the welcoming of the unclean, the presence of God in God's nonempirical activity.

Yet Jesus' own language in the end betrayed him. While he avoided speaking about God as a King, the use of empire (*basileia*) inevitably invoked a semantic system at odds with his own point of view. Linguistically Jesus' problem is easy to understand. He is dealing with three terms, with the primary term suppressed. The model of the parable is not A is like B, but A is like B is like C.

A (something unexpressed) is like B (the empire of God) is like C (leaven which a woman took). In most metaphorical systems the A term is abstract and receives its structure from the B term. But here empire of God has its own implied metaphorical system. Jesus attempted to control that system in two ways.

- By invoking a seldom-used variant of that system, speaking of the empire of God rather than the more common God as king.
- By using his parables to structure the symbol's meaning, perception, and experience.

But he failed. Soon the structure of empire began to dictate the meaning of the parables and to override and rewrite them. The parable of the Leaven in the Gospel of Thomas clearly demonstrates this semantic adulteration.

> The kingdom of the Father is like a certain woman. She took a little leaven, [concealed] it in some dough, and made it into large loaves.

While much ink has been spilt on the inversion of woman and leaven, probably to no avail, more interesting aspects have gone unnoticed. The reference to three measures is dropped, and with it the specific resonance to the tradition of the prophecy of the birth of Isaac. When Thomas introduces the contrast between little and large, the metaphorical structure of empire is asserting itself. Since empires are large and great, the motion from little to large sets up a metaphorical structure appropriate for an empire, and the story must end with great loaves, not leavening (corrupting) everything. Ironically, but not surprisingly, the Thomas version became the traditional interpretation of the parable, and Jesus' version was lost to ear.

But the subversive aspects of the metaphorical structure of empire extend well beyond the reinterpretation and rewriting of this parable. All the parables soon received either explicitly or implicitly appropriate imperial interpretations.

- The mustard plant became a real tree.
- The Samaritan became a good hero and not a threat.
- The father welcomes back the prodigal and rejects the elder son.
- The treasure becomes a gift of joy.
- The shrewd manager gets several new endings.
- The king becomes God who mercifully forgives while we ignore his blatant cruelty and lack of forgiveness.
- And so on.

Even more, the model for Jesus himself became imperial, so that the imperial titles of the Roman emperor more and more came to be applied to Jesus. At first this was probably ironic, as one can see for example in the application of "savior of the world" to Jesus at the conclusion of the Samaritan Woman at the Well story in the Gospel of John (4:42). In a small village in Samaria, a woman of dubious reputation entertains Jesus and the village folk first designate him "savior of the world," a title of the Roman imperial cult. Samaria is certainly an inappropriate place for Jesus to be proclaimed savior. But before long the irony is lost. And with Constantine, Jesus becomes a real savior with the Roman emperor making obeisance to him.

To take the historical Jesus seriously is to take his language seriously, to take his social context seriously, and to take seriously both his linguistic problem and his failure to overcome that problem. At the peril of modernizing Jesus, to take Jesus seriously is to see that he was betrayed by language. What he was actually talking about was so deep that language broke down.

Then again maybe we should see Jesus in the tradition of Job or Qoheleth or Jonah, although even these are too elite for Jesus. They indicate within the Jewish tradition a deep struggling to understand God's activity. I would suggest that what we have not attended to is Jesus' problem. To take Jesus seriously is to try to understand what motivated this language and activity, what problem set it in motion. That problem is ultimately symbolized by Jesus' effort to create a new language, a new metaphorical system in which to structure the experience of God, to re-imagine the world, to re-imagine the possibility of life itself.

Jesus as rebel

One of the most perplexing problems in the quest for the historical Jesus is why Jesus opted for such a radical program. People frequently finesse this problem by invoking the inevitability of history: What happened had to happen. But, of course, that is not true; it is the fallacy of the inevitable. Like most peasants in his situation, Jesus could have sat back and done nothing. At other times, I suspect, an assumed Christology warrants his confrontational stance. Unthinkingly we fall back on faith commitments as though those explain why he chose so revolutionary an agenda.

What complicates any attempt to solve the problem is the very lack of data. We know almost nothing about Jesus' interior life, his psychological or social development. Nor do we possess even a chronological narrative in which to arrange a "life of Jesus."

Social science methods have not provided a way forward. John Dominic Crossan, for example, presents in his *The Historical Jesus: The Life of a Mediterranean Jewish Peasant* a model of brokerage in the Roman Empire that produced a system on the verge of breakdown. But what Crossan has explained is why the Roman Empire was such an unstable society and why the Jews revolted in 68CE. What a social model cannot explain is why an individual decides to revolt. Social sciences deal with groups, not individuals.

Jesus' revolt takes a very special form. He revolts in parable. I see no evidence that Jesus was leading a political revolution or that he had a social program in mind. He clearly affected the lives of people, but he was not a social organizer or activist. Although the idea is now out of fashion, Jesus the oral storyteller seems to me closer to a poet. The activist will always be dissatisfied with the poetic vision, but change comes about because a creative individual has that vision.

At times it seems to me that it is easier to know what Jesus is against than what he is for. To borrow a term from computer science, Jesus' vision is against the default world, especially insofar as the default world is oppressive and destructive of the life of what he calls the poor. He is opposed to the purity code and the imperial order as models for God. He is not simply a contrarian, but oftentimes it is easier to make clear what one stands against than just exactly what one stands for.

Seamus Heaney has recently addressed this issue in his *The Redress of Poetry*. I take the liberty of quoting a passage that is to the point.

> And in the activity of poetry too, there is a tendency to place a coun-ter-reality in the scales — a reality which may be only imagined but which nevertheless has weight because it is imagined within the grav-itational pull of the actual and can therefore hold its own and bal-ance out against the historical situation. This redressing effect of poetry comes from its being a glimpsed alternative, a revelation of potential that is denied or constantly threatened by circumstances. And sometimes, of course, it happens that such a revelation, once enshrined in the poem, remains as a standard for the poet, so that he or she must then submit to the strain of bearing witness in his or her own life to the place of consciousness established in the poem (pp. 3–4).

In his explanation of how poetry functions, Heaney brings out a number of points that are critical to understanding how Jesus' para-bles and aphorisms operated. Jesus' vision is not an alternative to the default world in the sense that it is a replacement. It is a counter-weight, a counter-reality, in Heaney's terms. Thus, it is always dia-logically related to that default world. The default world will almost always win in the long run, because it is the default. That is why Jesus' own language betrayed him in the end.

Jesus' parables are "a glimpsed alternative, a revelation of potential that is denied or constantly threatened by circumstance," or in my terms, constantly threatened by the default world. A glimpsed alternative is not a worked out program. It is always temporary, glimpsed. It is a possibility, not a reality.

Once enshrined in parable, it remains a standard for the poet, or in this case Jesus. Thus the empire of God is not what drives Jesus, but the glimpse enshrined in the parable that is likened to the empire of God. It is an alternative reality only as a counter-balance to the real reality, whether the Roman Empire or the Temple state. As Heaney remarks, the poet "must then submit to the strain of bearing witness in his or her own life to the place of consciousness established in the poem." In Jesus' parables his consciousness is established and his life bears witness to that. Thus the parables provide the coordinates for understanding Jesus' deeds.

A problem with this view of Jesus is that it runs counter to the assumption that he is the founder of a new religion. This demands something new and complete, not something in counter-balance, not just a glimpse. Such a view of Jesus appears too ephemeral for what came afterwards: Christianity and the church triumphant. With my view, Jesus remains firmly attached to Judaism and is engaged in an argument within Judaism. He is part of a continuing debate. To put it too boldly, he is against the Deuteronomist and sides with Job and Qohelet.

To return to Heaney's argument, poetry is a redress because it envisions "a reality which may be only imagined but which nevertheless has weight because it is imagined within the gravitational pull of the actual and can therefore hold its own and balance out against the historical situation." The redress of the parable is hope and hope has power, not because it is a concrete program, a worked out plan or blueprint, but because it creates the counter-reality to the default moral world. It says things do not have to be this way.

Václav Havel was imprisoned for his poems and plays, led the velvet revolution, and became the first President of Czechoslovakia and then the Czech Republic. What Havel has to say about hope explains how parables and the empire of God functioned as a revolutionary symbol for Jesus and his followers. Hope, he says, is

a state of mind, not a state of the world . . . and it's not essentially dependent on some particular observation of the world or estimate of the situation . . . it transcends the world that is immediately experienced, and is anchored somewhere beyond its horizons . . . It is not the conviction that something will turn out well, but the certainty that something makes sense, regardless of how it turns out. (p. 181)

It is no accident that those who espouse an apocalyptic Jesus avoid the parables. You cannot get from the parables to an apocalyptic Jesus, although you can get from an apocalyptic Jesus to an apocalyptic interpretation of the parables. But such an interpretation is the default moral world, because apocalyptic is the Deuteronomist's vision as the future divine fact. From an apocalyptic Jesus one does get to the founder of Christianity.

Heaney has captured in his understanding of the redress of poetry an insight into how Jesus' language offered to his audience an alternative to the world in which they were trapped — a world burdened by purity laws segregating the unclean from the clean and into further degrees of purity or shame. A world where those on the bottom are imprisoned in unchangeable structures and await a divine solution. A world in which enemies threaten at every point. Jesus in his language offers a counter world, a vision, an openness to experience. It is a "glimpsed alternative, a revelation of potential that is denied or constantly threatened by circumstances." It may be only an imagined or re-imagined alternative, but it derives its weight from its opposition to and careful observation of the historical world. Apart from the gravitational pull of that historical world, it is without meaning or open to whatever one wants it to mean.

Jesus revolts in parable and the parables create a counter-world, a hoped-for world that redresses the world as it is and surely makes sense, regardless of how it turns out, even it if turns out to be his crucifixion.

⇒ Epilogue ⇐

Living in a Re-imagined World

A substantial bar to making the parables applicable today is the great distance between them and us. Jesus was a first century, Jewish, Galilean peasant and his concerns, speech, and idioms belong to that culture. We belong to a very different world. The transition is difficult, like the transition from Homer to us, or even from Shakespeare to us. Yet the parables do invoke universal themes.

I propose the following question: Can you base your life on the re-imagined world of the parables? My answer to this question is a resounding "Yes," but to explain it I will have to relate a little bit of my own story.

Before we begin, recall the three coordinates around which in the last chapter I developed a comprehensive view of Jesus' parables, sayings, and deeds.

- God is unclean.
- God is present in absence, not apocalyptic resolution.
- Cooperation, not contest, is the basis for the Empire of God.

These three coordinates for me summarize the re-imagined world of the parables, or to put it another way, they triangulate the empire of God.

Community of Hope

The Community of Hope (COH) began in Tulsa, OK, in 1993 as a ministry of outreach to those with HIV/AIDS. The model for the

Community's life was drawn from the base communities in Central and South America, adapted for urban life in North America. Because its principal outreach was to those suffering from HIV/AIDS, it soon became a magnet for gays and lesbians seeking a religious life.

COH was sponsored by the United Methodist Church and its founding pastor, Leslie Penrose, was a United Methodist Minister. The arrival of a new bishop some time later made life increasingly difficult for COH within the United Methodist fold. When the pastor was forced to resign as a United Methodist Minister, COH began a search for a new denominational home, eventually covenanting with the United Church of Christ. Behind this bare historical outline lies a tragic tale which will not be told here.

A number of years ago my life was in crisis but I was coping. My confidence in the institutional church of my birth had failed, although my confidence in religion remained high. Leslie Penrose, a former student of mine, invited me to give a series of presentations on Jesus' parables to the recently started Community of Hope.

I went for four weeks and have remained for eight years.

What I found was a community where the parables formed the heart and soul of the Community's life, although the Community is not always explicit about this. From them I have seen how the dynamic of the parables works its way through the life of a community.

Leaven

I frequently draw on the parable of the Leaven with church groups because it gives such a powerful insight into Jesus' vision. But usually the parable scares congregations. They can't believe their ears. They find it blasphemous. The reason is simple. Most middle class Americans, those who inhabit the world of the mainline Christian churches, belong to the default world against which the parable is re-imagining the empire of God. They intuitively sense that they are the parable's target.

The Community of Hope immediately sensed what was at stake because the parable related their life story. As gays and lesbians, they were the leaven of this society. Many had been asked to leave a church, or at least had felt unwelcome and judged. Many, through a long journey from self-hatred to self-acceptance, had at last come to see that they were not cursed or an abomination, but loved and cherished by God — even when their churches told them otherwise. For them, the Leaven was their story.

As one said, "the kingdom of God is like a queer . . ."

Empire of God

Just as Jesus' parables, saying, and deeds frequently exposed the arbitrariness of his society's barriers, so too COH is about breaking down barriers. One of the principal barriers that the Community must attack is the formidable one the church represents to many of its members. Most have experienced exclusion and yet still have a deep sense of the need for religion and spirituality. They understand the toxic aspect of religion, the seductiveness implicit in the parable of the Treasure.

While old barriers are being torn down, new boundaries need to be built up, not to exclude, but to protect. The Community at worship becomes a safe place for truth telling. It becomes a place where they can be "out," even though they may not be out otherwise in public. It becomes a place where they can tell their stories and discover who they are. During Joys and Concerns I hear about folks' medical progress, depressions, struggles, alcoholism. The list is almost interminable. Sometimes when I had thought I had a bad week, I discovered that by comparison my week was pretty good. AIDS has a way of putting things in perspective.

One Sunday stands out. A young woman who was confined to a wheelchair said that her joy was that she was at church, and her concern was that she had been raped two nights before. She had called a member of COH and several folks took care of her immediately. What impressed me was her courage and freedom to announce this in public. I could not think of another church where this could be publicly dealt with at worship.

I have wrestled most of my scholarly life with what Jesus was getting at in using the phrase empire of God. Whether in my own writing or that of other scholars I never had the sense that the empire of God, the kingdom of God, or God's imperial rule — however we translate it — was a reality. It existed in the head, as a theological idea.

In community as safe space I discovered the empire of God at work. At COH the empire of God is safe space for the world's leaven. That's what happened in the ministry of Jesus. His speech and deeds created a safe space for those who were poor, a space where for that brief period of time the Roman Empire or the purity code or whatever could not intrude and dominate. That's why he describes the empire of God as "right there in your presence" (Luke 17:21) or "inside and outside you" and "spread out upon the earth and people don't see it" (Thomas 113). That's also why it's an empire — it is fortified, safe space.

Journey

The metaphor or metaphors that a group uses to express itself not only represent its self understanding but also shape that understanding. A mighty fortress is one such image; onward Christian soldiers calls up another.

The dominant metaphor at COH is journey because the life of the Community is a pilgrimage, an ongoing voyage of discovery. Where that journey is leading the Community is unknown. This is one of a number of places where COH has deliberately chosen a non-apocalyptic vision of its life.

The Community has no membership but only companions on the journey. Those who wish to companion with the Community paint their hands in rainbow colors and put the imprint on the wall. All decisions in the Community's life are done by consensus, not voting. The imperial structure typical of most church life has been thoroughly abandoned.

All this became problematic after the United Methodists forced COH to leave, and when eventually the Community joined the United Church of Christ, the UCC advisors found it difficult to understand an organization that had no committees, no structure of power. "Who makes the decisions?" was the constant refrain. "We do." "But what if you disagree?" "Then we work it out. That's what it means to be on a journey together." "How do you know when a decision has been made?" "When the Community publicly affirms its decision."

The advisors thought it was admirable that for each dollar we take in we give half of it away, but they thought it was imprudent for a Community always on the brink of financial disaster to be so lavish with its funds. (The community puts its faith not in scarcity, but abundance — only of a different kind.) And not having a membership roll raised real bureaucratic concern about how many votes COH would have in denominational meetings and assessment. Eventually the Community telephone directory served the purpose.

If you are going to take the parable of the Samaritan and its coordinates seriously, then life has to be reconsidered, for it can no longer involve power-over-another. It is perhaps easier for those without power to do this re-imagining than those of us used to wielding power. As a white, straight male I find it stimulating and threatening to be always in the minority. It's a position I'm not used to.

Death

With so many companions of COH with AIDS, death is a constant visitor, although not as frequently now as in the early years. The new drugs have made a critical difference. But no one knows how long they will continue to work and whether AIDS may again begin rapidly to claim its victims.

Part of the culture of Tulsa, Oklahoma, is Oral Roberts and Kenneth Hagan with their "expect-a-miracle" religion. This charismatic, apocalyptic version of Christianity insists that if you only have faith, God will work a miracle. Of course, the catch twenty-two is that if you are sick and no miracle comes, then your lack of faith is the problem. This culture infests our city.

Many with HIV/AIDS both see their condition as a curse from God and expect or want a miracle. Part of the strength of the COH is its ability to help folks see that neither of these is reasonable. AIDS is not God's punishment and there will be no miracle. Rather God is present with us in the suffering.

I have watched folks with AIDS die holy deaths, yet I'm sure many good and religious persons would see their deaths as God's punishment for their "life styles."

Scott had been a successful businessman and a long distance runner. He appeared financially well off. Over the years I knew him AIDS began to ravage his body more and more and the new cocktail drugs did not work. With his immune system so vulnerable, he developed cancer, and I took him to many of his chemotherapy treatments. I was never sure why he wanted me to take him, but he consistently asked for me.

He was religiously much more conservative than I, but there is a lot of religious diversity in COH and for the most part it works. We talked about many things, with me mostly listening. His health was always topic number one, and as chemo failed, he spoke more and more about when enough was enough. The treatments became more invasive, more terrorizing, more disabling. Scott concluded that when life becomes nothing more than fighting the disease, maybe it's time to stop.

He made the decision to stop chemotherapy and all of his other medicines. Several days later, Scott was dead.

Scott was a holy man. He was also a homosexual. The apparent disjunction in this conjunction is the mystery of the empire of God.

Both Jesus and early Christians found family a difficult issue, a well kept secret in these days of family values. Many gays and lesbians have wonderful supportive families, but many more do not. At the Community of Hope I learned to distinguish between given families — our families of birth — and chosen families. The empire of God as safe space was almost bound to lead Jesus into conflict with his own given family. Marginalization does that to folks. Families are about maintaining established boundaries. The empire of God is about chosen family. "Here are my mother and my brothers. For whoever does the will of my Father in Heaven, that's my brother and sister and mother" (Matt 12:49–50; Thomas 99). As the saying about hating your father and mother (Luke 14:26) indicates, early Christianity's experience with families was conflictive. Ironically family is a frequent model for the church in the New Testament. The need to form family, even chosen family, is strong. This bond is as strong as blood.

The miracle in Scott's life was the chosen family gathered around him at his death and his funeral. He touched the lives of many, was there for many. All the years he was dying, he devoted his life to others. He had started a food pantry for those with HIV/AIDS and volunteered extensively in the community at large. As we waited for the hospice workers to come, his concern was for those who were in need of his help.

Scott's religion had taught him to expect a miracle. HIV/AIDS taught him that would not happen. Scott's religion had taught him that homosexuality was evil; the Community of Hope helped him discover otherwise. Though without the hope of a miracle, he did not die hopeless. He found hope in reaching out to others, in serving others, and in the comfort of his given and chosen family.

Christianity without Christ

My experience in the Community of Hope has provided me with what I sometimes view as a laboratory where I have seen the parables work their miracle. But the power of the parables to constitute community raises certain fundamental questions about the future of Christianity. What they perhaps call for is a radical reformation.

The parables raise fundamental questions about how we imagine or re-imagine the world and Jesus' place in that re-imagined world. One of the reasons I have told my story of the Community of Hope is that I see there the living out of the re-imagined world of the parables. Not perfectly, of course; the parables don't imagine a perfect world but a master and his manager.

Just as Jesus is not the topic of parables, we need a Christianity without Christ. The question we should be asking is not who Christ is, but the nature of the God Jesus hides in his parables. I use "hide" deliberately because God is no more the explicit topic of the parables than Jesus.

The parables thus force another radical question: Why trust this re-imagined world? Why trust Jesus?

There are several ways to preempt the asking of these questions. The two most prominent are an appeal to the authority of scripture and Christology.

Authority

The authority of scripture is a question that is tearing many churches (and much of American society) apart. "God wrote it, the Bible says it, I believe it" is a bumper sticker I've often seen. Such a slogan is hard to argue with. It seems so simple, so straightforward. Yet not even the most literal of literalists takes everything in the Bible literally. We are selectively literalist; we all make exceptions when doing so fits our position. We no longer demand an eye for an eye, nor do we pluck our eye out when it offends us. Most have found ways to accommodate Genesis' story of creation either by interpreting it metaphorically or rationalizing it as scientific. The list could go on and on. It only shows that the authority of scripture is selective, not absolute.

A simplistic belief in the authority of scripture hides a more fundamental authority issue: by what authority do we venerate the few scriptural passages we choose to take literally? The authority of scripture is a circular problem from which there is no escape. The problem with the authority of scripture is who gets to determine what is authoritative? Over such issues the Reformation was started and continues.

Jesus' Place

Obviously Jesus is at the center of Christianity — or is he? For over a hundred years now theologians have debated this question under the rubric of the Christ of faith and the Jesus of history. One basic argument is that we do not come to faith by studying history but by the preaching about Christ in the church. We come to faith not as historians but as believers within a community. This, of course, is true. But it misses the point. Our faith is not a single moment of coming to faith or conversion, but an ongoing activity or process. Our faith grows and develops in response to our concrete experience. A major component of that growth is intellectual, coming to awareness that we are people with a history and are determined by our history. So we begin to question,

- Just who was Jesus historically?
- What can we really know about him?
- How does that comport with the Christ of faith? with what I was taught?
- Should not the Christ of faith and the Jesus of history be at least compatible?

The response to this line of questioning is usually that faith grants certainty, while history deals only in possibilities and probabilities. Again, this misunderstands both faith and history. We need faith for what we don't know or can't know. Faith is a gamble about what might be, not what certainly is. If faith is certain, it is not faith but knowledge.

In one way the fundamentalists have it correct. They insist that Jesus is the center and that there is no distinction between Jesus and the Christ. But to accomplish this, they avoid history because that will not give them the Jesus they demand. Yet instinctively they and most of us know that the gap between the Jesus of history and the Christ of faith should be as small as possible.

- If faith is in Christ, whose Christ is it? Again we are back to the problem of authority.

• If faith is in Christ, how do we know that Christ is not substantially the projection or construction of some authority?

• If the historical Jesus is somehow the ground of our faith, whose historical Jesus is the ground?

Since history is always in the process of revision, it can never reach a final answer. But that is like life itself. Most of our answers are provisional. The historical Jesus, like the real Jesus of Nazareth, is a moving target. At every point we are thrown back onto our own decisions. There is no unconditional starting point exempt from historical relativity.

Christology, defining the Christ, attempts to short-circuit the question by making Jesus one with God and thus investing him with authority: You must believe this because Jesus is God and God must be obeyed.

Faithfulness

Ultimately we have faith not *in* Jesus, but faith *with* Jesus. In the re-imagined world of the parables we stand beside Jesus and trust that his world will work, that it can provide the safe space — the empire of God — that resists all other empires. Jesus is our companion on the journey, not our Lord and Master. The parables lead us to the conviction of the reality of this imagined world. Like Jesus, we can be faithful to the vision of the parable.

This shift from faith *in* to *with* is not as innovative as it might sound. In recent years a fierce debate has raged in Pauline studies over the phrase "faith in Jesus," the traditional English translation of *pistis tou Christou*. Recently, important Pauline scholars have argued that the phrase should be translated "Jesus' faithfulness." They argue that Paul did not maintain we were saved by faith in Jesus but by Jesus' faithfulness. We can quickly grasp what is at stake by comparing the NRSV translation of Romans 3:26 to the one suggested by Stanley Stowers.

NRSV	Stowers
it was to prove at the present time that he himself is righteous and that he justifies the one who has faith in Jesus.	He did this to prove his own loving justice at this crisis in history so as to be just and to make right the person whose status springs from Jesus' faithfulness.

In the traditional translation represented by the NRSV, clearly faith in Jesus is what saves, whereas in Stowers's translation Jesus' faithfulness is what confers the status of being made right.

This new understanding of Paul presses the question we have been pursuing: To what was Jesus faithful? My argument is that Jesus was faithful to the re-imagined world of the parables. The quote from the poet Seamus Heaney from the last chapter captures perfectly this aspect of faithfulness: "And sometimes, of course, it happens that such a revelation, once enshrined in the poem, remains as a standard for the poet, so that he or she must then submit to the strain of bearing witness in his or her own life to the place of consciousness established in the poem."

Jesus' life bears witness to the re-imagined world of the parables. It established for him and those who followed him a new consciousness, a new way of being in the world. Such a consciousness represents for me a new foundation for Christianity. To be more accurate, it represents for me a return to the original basis for the resurrection. Those who had faith in the parable's re-imagined world proclaimed him still alive because of their faithfulness to that re-imagined world.

The parable is always a counterweight to the default world, and as such it imagines a counterweighted God. The God Jesus hides in the parables identifies with a polluted world, not the world of the temple; Adonai's presence is discovered in absence, not apocalyptic revenge; and G-d's empire is based not on shame and honor, not on patron and client, not on contest — but on cooperation. The risk in such a counter weighted world is that the power of other empires is mighty indeed. Since the counter-world of the parable is always an imagined world, the real world is always there, always threatening to destroy that world of imagination. But faithfulness demands living out that risk by re-imagining with Jesus the parables once again.

An Essay on Parables

Early parable studies

We can divide the history of parable studies into two stages. The initial stage began with Adolf Jülicher's *Die Gleichnisreden Jesu* (1910). Of primary importance was his rejection of allegory, which had long dominated the interpretation of parables. He did this by arguing that parables had one point, not multiple points as in allegory. For Jülicher that one point was a moral point. His careful studies of how parables fit into their gospel contexts demonstrated that the fit was poor. Those who challenge his attack on allegory by pointing to rabbinic parables, some of which did receive allegorical interpretations, have always overlooked this aspect of Jülicher's work. He clearly demonstrates that the allegories in the gospels are not the original interpretations of the parables.

> **Gain:** *Rejection of allegory*
> **Gain:** *Parables not dependent on their Gospel context*

In 1935 the British scholar C.H. Dodd published his Schaffer Lectures given at Yale under the title of *The Parables of the Kingdom.* Dodd followed in the steps of Jülicher, but instead of his single moral point, Dodd shifted the debate to eschatology. For him, the parables were about "realized eschatology." They proclaimed a kingdom that was already here, anticipating in many ways the conclusions of the Jesus Seminar.

Dodd also produced one of the most influential definitions of parable:

At its simplest the parable is a metaphor or simile drawn from nature or common life, arresting the hearer by its vividness or stangeness, and leaving the mind in sufficient doubt about its precise application to tease it into active thought (p. 16).

Gain: *Introduced the question of the parables' eschatology.*

By far the most important parable scholar of the post World War II era was the German scholar Joachim Jeremias. The German edition of his work went through eight editions, and there were two revised English translations, with the final revision based on the eighth German edition. Jeremias is directly dependent on Dodd, but even more he depends on the insights of the form critics, especially Rudolf Bultmann. The form critics had begun to study the development of the oral tradition of Jesus' sayings, and Jeremias developed the laws of transmission for the parables. These rules allowed Jeremias to reconstruct the original words of Jesus, often attempting to make guesses about the Aramaic text he believed was behind the Greek.

Like the form critics he thought the interpretation of a parable was determined by its life situation (*Sitz im Leben*), its original context. For Jeremias this specific situation for most of the parables was Jesus' debate with the Pharisees.

Jeremias was the first parable scholar to deal with the parables in the Gospel of Thomas as an independent witness to the parables of Jesus.

While Jeremias developed the insights of the form critics, his theological position was much more conservative. Bultmann thought Jesus was the presupposition of New Testament theology. For Jeremias "We stand right before Jesus when reading his parables" (12). Jeremias stresses an eschatology that is both realized, "Now is the Day of Salvation," and yet to come, "The Imminence of Catastrophe."

Gain: *Outlined the stages for a history of the parables from Jesus to the Gospels.*

Bultmann, Rudolf. *The History of the Synoptic Tradition.* Translated by John Marsh. New York: Harper & Row, 1963 (1919).

Dodd, C.H. *The Parables of the Kingdom.* New York: Charles Scribner's Sons, 1935, 1961.

Jeremias, Joachim. *The Parables of Jesus.* Translated by S.H. Hooke. New York: Charles Scribner's Sons, 1972.

Jülicher, Adolf. *Die Gleichnisreden Jesu.* 2 vols. Tübingen: J.C.B. Mohr [Paul Siebeck], 1910, reprinted Darmstadt: Wissenschaftliche Buchgesellschaft, 1969.

The American shift

Beginning in the 1960's scholarship on the parables became an American enterprise and has remained such. Robert Funk and Dan Via, independently of each other, instigated a new approach to the parables that was as revolutionary as Jülicher's rejection of allegory. Literary studies had a long and strong history in American English departments and both Funk and Via drew heavily on this tradition of scholarship.

Via redefined the parable as an "aesthetic object." In this way he was attempting to overcome the limitations of historical criticism as practiced by Jeremias and others. Since it is impossible to determine the original situation (*Sitz im Leben*) of any of the parables, a strict historical understanding is hopeless. Historical factors should be taken into consideration only insofar as demanded by the narrative. The rejection of the necessity to know or reconstruct the specific occasion for a parable liberated interpretation. This position is not anti-historical, but redefines the place of history in interpretation.

For Via "The only important consideration is the internal meaning of the work itself" (p. 77). Here we notice the decisive influence of the New Criticism with it's emphasis on the poem as autonomous. As an aesthetic object the parable is not "time-conditioned" as are non-literary texts. Like literary artistic artifacts, the parable is "untranslatable." The original hearers "were no more able to translate them completely into other terms than we are" (p. 32).

> **Gain:** *The specific historical situation does not determine meaning, or the meaning of a parable cannot be reduced to a specific situation in the ministry of Jesus.*

Funk took Dodd's definition of parable and expanded it in a chapter entitled "The Parable as Metaphor" in his *Language, Hermeneutics and the Word of God.* Metaphor became the way Funk explored the parables. Highly dependent on the British scholar Owen Barfield,

Funk contrasts the logic of discursive language and metaphorical language. Whereas ordinary or discursive language makes explicit, metaphorical language creates meaning. "To say *A is B* is a metaphor, which, because of the juxtaposition of two discrete and not entirely comparable entities, produces an impact upon the imagination and induces a vision of that which cannot be conveyed by prosaic or discursive speech" (p. 136). The juxtaposition that is inherent in metaphor "raises the potential for new meaning" (p. 138). Metaphor with its potential to create new meaning "reveals a mystery: the mystery of kaleidoscopic reality directly apprehended" (p. 140).

Funk's expansion of the definition of parable as metaphor has proven fertile and dynamic in the interpretation of parables, both in his own work and the work of others. In his first book, *Language, Hermeneutics and the Word of God*, he explored the parable of the Good Samaritan in a truly brilliant fashion. Since the author of the Gospel of Luke had first tied the parable to the question of who is my neighbor, the parable had been understood as an example story — this was how you were to be a good neighbor, like the Samaritan. Funk first showed that this was a gentile version of the story which turned the Samaritan into a literal example and missed the metaphorical possibilities of "Samaritan." He joins Via in rejecting the necessity of knowing the specific occasion for the parable in order to understand it.

> When it is asked why Jesus chose the Samaritan as the central figure in the parable, it is simply not satisfactory to answer that the Samaritan is merely a model of neighborliness. For in that case the parable is reduced to a commonplace and its bite completely vitiated. Rather, the Samaritan is he whom the victim does not, could not expect would help, indeed does not want help from. The literal, i.e., historical, significance of the Samaritan is what gives the parable its edge. In this respect the Samaritan is a *secular* figure. . . On the other hand, the Samaritan is brought into a constellation in which he cannot be anticipated. It is this surprising, odd turn which shatters the realism, the everydayness of the story. A narrative begun with all the traits of an experience about which everyone knows, or thinks he knows, is ruptured at the crucial juncture by a factor which does not square with everyday experience. The "logic" of everydayness is broken upon the "logic" of the parable. It is the juxtaposition of the two logics that turns the Samaritan, and hence the parable, into a metaphor (p. 213).

In Jesus as Precursor Funk explored two more parables. In "The Parable of the Leaven: Away-From-Here as the Destination" he showed how the very terms of the parable established a metaphorical meaning at variance with the traditional understanding of the parable. The Leaven, as a symbol for moral corruption demanded to be taken on its own terms. In "The Looking-Glass Tree is for the Birds" he showed how the Mustard Seed parable burlesques the expectations of the great cedar of Lebanon.

> **Gain:** *Parables function as a metaphorical structure or system.*
> **Gain:** *Attention must be paid to the very metaphorical nature of the words themselves, eg., Leaven, Samaritan.*

Both Via and Funk made real gains in the interpretation of the parables by accenting their literary character. In *Jesus as Precursor* Funk attempted to draw the parables into conversation with other poets, especially Kafka. John Dominic Crossan, one of the most creative New Testament scholars of the last quarter of the 20th century, in a number of books explored and expanded the insights of Funk and Via. Crossan's work was not revolutionary like Funk and Via's, but it consolidated their gains, made them readily accessible to a wider audience, especially in *Dark Interval* and *In Parables*, and furthered the exploration of literary method.

Crossan's thesis is that "Jesus is proclaiming what might be termed *permanent eschatology*, the permanent presence of God as the one who challenges world and shatters its complacency repeatedly" (*In Parables*, p. 26). Crossan organizes the parables under three headings dealing with the kingdom's temporality: "its *advent* as gift of God, its *reversal* of the recipient's world, and its empowering to life and *action*" (p. 36).

Jeremias had been concerned with recovering the very words of Jesus (*ipsissima verba*), even at times trying to translate back into the Aramaic. But such is an impossibility because it assumes that the parables of Jesus existed from the beginning as written (really printed) text. In *Cliffs of Fall* Crossan sharply attacked this notion and demonstrated that in orality what is remembered is not the words themselves, but the structure (*ipsissima structura*), the form, the pattern.

Crossan also pursued Funk's initial efforts to relate the parables to other poets. His *Raid on the Articulate: Comic Eschatology in Jesus and Borges*, is as the title indicates, an extended analysis of both Jesus and Borges. It turns out that Borges throws a great deal of light on Jesus.

> **Gain:** *We are dealing not with the very words of Jesus but with the structure (the memory and performance) of the parables.*

My own book, *Hear Then the Parable*, follows in the tradition of Funk, Via, and Crossan. It was the first book since Jülicher to deal with all the parables. It draws heavily from studies on the differences between orality and literacy, develops a comprehensive literary strategy based on reader-response criticism. This enables me to ask not so much what Jesus intended, but what effect the parable had on its audience, accenting the dialogic character of the parable. Finally, I introduced into the conversation social science methods as a way of developing the repertoire of a text, those social conventions and assumptions that the teller and audience hold in common.

One of the more important developments in New Testament criticism in the last twenty years has been the use of insights derived from social sciences. William Herzog's *Parables as Subversive Speech: Jesus as Pedagogue of the Oppressed* has pursued parables in this light. For him the parables encode first century structures of oppression. Herzog often produces illuminating readings of the parables, making sense of details that have often left one confused. But his antagonism to literary criticism seems unwarranted. Social world theories and literary theories are not opposed, but need to be used hand in hand. The parable is a *narrative* which *encodes a special social order*. Understanding narrative demands a literary method and explaining the encoding of the social order requires the social sciences.

> **Gain:** *Literary method and social science method are both necessary to interpret the parables.*

David Gowler's little *What Are They Saying About Parables?* is a helpful guide to the history of the parable interpretation. It covers the whole field in much more detail than I have and is generally fair and reliable. My one criticism is that since he does not help the reader sort through the options, parable interpretation appears chaotic. Seen from the outside, maybe it is.

Crossan, Dominic. *In Parables: The Challenge of the Historical Jesus*. New York: Harper and Row, 1973. Reprint, Sonoma, CA: Polebridge Press, 1992.

_____. *The Dark Interval, Towards a Theology of Story*. Niles, IL: Argus Communications, 1975. Reprint, Sonoma, CA: Polebridge Press, 1988.

_____. *Raid on the Articulate: Comic Eschatology in Jesus and Borges*. New York: Harper and Row, 1976.

_____. *Finding Is the First Act*. Semeia Supplements. Philadelphia: Fortress Press, 1979.

_____. *Cliffs of Fall: Paradox and Polyvalence in the Parables of Jesus*. New York: Seabury, 1980.

Funk, Robert W. *Language, Hermeneutic and Word of God*. New York: Harper and Row, 1966.

_____. *Jesus as Precursor*, Semeia Supplements. Philadelphia: Fortress Press, 1975; reprinted Sonoma, CA: Polebridge Press, 1994.

Gowler, David. *What Are They Saying About Parables?* Mahwah: Paulist Press, 2000.

Herzog, William R. III. *Parables as Subversive Speech: Jesus as Pedagogue of the Oppressed*. Louisville: Westminster/John Knox, 1994.

Scott, Bernard Brandon. *Hear Then the Parable, a Commentary on the Parables of Jesus*. Minneapolis: Fortress Press, 1989.

Via, Dan. *The Parables: Their Literary and Existential Dimension*. Philadelphia: Fortress Press, 1967.

Historical Jesus studies

The larger context into which parable studies fit is the quest for the historical Jesus, but unfortunately recent studies have moved away from the parables, in my judgment at a loss to those studies. We are now in a new, third stage of quests for the historical Jesus. I have written a rather comprehensive study of the three stages and I recommend it to the reader. Here I will only point to some of the more important recent studies.

By far the most important work in this new wave is John Dominic Crossan's *The Historical Jesus: The Life of a Mediterranean Jewish Peasant*. He may be the Strauss of our generation, and his book the one that defines the study for the next generation. Crossan proposes a comprehensive method for isolating the sayings that come from Jesus, a strategy that departs from the traditional criteria for authenticity. He is very strong on how the Roman Empire sets the overall context in which to understand Jesus, and is highly dependent upon the social science findings.

E.P. Sanders in *Jesus and Judaism* probably gets the honor for initiating the new stage. He moves away from the words of Jesus because he is skeptical about the possibility of discovering their meaning. Via,

Funk, and Scott scare him. Instead he posits ten deeds of Jesus that must have happened and then deduces from them the eschatology (temple restoration) that he sees implied in them. Needless to say, Sanders' ten indisputable facts did not turn out to be so indisputable.

Marcus Borg has been the great popularizer of this new stage of the quest. Much to his credit he has been able to converse with those for whom much of the debate is incomprehensible. He has faced head on the question of eschatology and argued persuasively that Jesus' eschatology was not apocalyptic but realized. He sees Jesus as "a charismatic who was a healer, sage, prophet, and revitalization movement founder" (1987: 15).

John Meier has written two large volumes with a third soon expected all under the title *A Marginal Jew*. In many ways Meier's approach and his Jesus are rather traditional. His historical method is not leavened by literary criticism nor the social sciences. I sometimes think this is the book that would have been written if the old quest had continued. Well, I guess it has. The treatment of the miracle tradition is supreme. He sets a benchmark that other scholars will have to acknowledge. To claim more than Meier does will be difficult.

The two reports of the Jesus Seminar, *The Five Gospels: The Search for the Authentic Words of Jesus* and *The Acts of Jesus: Search for the Authentic Deeds of Jesus* do not add up to a full blown study of Jesus. They don't tell you what Jesus meant or was about. But they do represent a consensus of what can be ascribed to Jesus. No other book about Jesus has more than one author on the title page. That Funk could get so many scholars to sign on to the final report is an achievement.

Finally, Stephen Patterson has written *The God of Jesus: The Historical Jesus and the Search for Meaning*, a very fine and readable book that is in many ways the best of what is available. He is not pioneering new methods. He pays careful attention to the data. This might be the place to start and is surely a book not to miss.

Borg, Marcus J. *Meeting Jesus Again for the First Time: The Historical Jesus and the Heart of Contemporary Faith*. San Francisco: HarperSanFrancisco, 1994.

———. *Jesus, a New Vision: Spirit, Culture, and the Life of Discipleship*. San Francisco: Harper and Row, 1987.

Crossan, John Dominic. *The Historical Jesus: The Life of a Mediterranean Jewish Peasant.* San Francisco: HarperSanFrancisco, 1991.

———. *Jesus: A Revolutionary Biography.* San Francisco: HarperSanFrancisco, 1994.

Funk, Robert W., Roy W. Hoover, and The Jesus Seminar, eds. *The Five Gospels: The Search for the Authentic Words of Jesus.* New York: Macmillan Publishing Company, 1993.

Funk, Robert W., and The Jesus Seminar, eds. *The Acts of Jesus: Search for the Authentic Deeds of Jesus.* San Francisco: HarperSanFrancisco, 1998.

Meier, John P. *A Marginal Jew: Rethinking the Historical Jesus.* 2 vols, The Anchor Bible Reference Library. Garden City: Doubleday, 1991, 1994.

Patterson, Stephen J. *The God of Jesus: The Historical Jesus and the Search for Meaning.* Harrisburg, PA: Trinity Press International, 1998.

Sanders, E.P. *Jesus and Judaism.* Philadelphia: Fortress Press, 1985.

———. *The Historical Figure of Jesus.* New York: Allen Lane, The Penguin Press, 1993.

Scott, Bernard Brandon. "New Options in an Old Quest." In *The Historical Jesus through Catholic and Jewish Eyes*, edited by Leonard J. Greenspoon, Dennis Hamm, S.J. and Bryan F. LeBeau, pp. 1–50. Harrisburg, PA: Trinity Press International, 2000.

Q and the Gospel of Thomas

For convenient translations of Q and the Gospel of Thomas, see Robert Miller, *The Complete Gospels.* *The Q Thomas Reader*, edited by John Kloppenborg and others, has translations, notes, and excellent introductions. *The Nag Hammadi Library in English*, edited by James M. Robinson, makes available all the texts of this important find.

Stephen Patterson's *The Gospel of Thomas and Jesus* is the best over all study of the Gospel of Thomas. I find his arguments for the independence of the Thomas tradition nuanced and convincing. Those who would assert the dependence of Thomas on the Synoptics need to disprove his arguments. Ron Cameron's "Parable Interpretation in the Gospel of Thomas" lays out the issues of Thomas as an interpreter of the parables.

Kloppenborg's *The Formation of Q* is a seminal work that initiated the modern study of Q. His recent *Excavating Q* is a magisterial work that not only answers his critics, but also advances and consolidates Q studies. This is the book to read. Arland Jacobson has provided in *The First Gospel* an accessible overview of Q.

The Critical Edition of Q, Edited by Robinson, Kloppenborg, and Paul Hoffman is an international effort modeled on the procedures of the Jesus Seminar to reach a consensus on the text of Q. Kloppenborg's own *Q Parallels* is a helpful study tool.

Cameron, Ron. "Parable Interpretation in the Gospel of Thomas." *Forum* 2 (1986): 3–40.
Jacobson, Arland. D. *The First Gospel, an Introduction to Q*. Sonoma, CA: Polebridge, 1992.
Kloppenborg, John S. *Q Parallels: Synopsis, Critical Notes & Concordance*, Facets & Foundations. Sonoma, CA: Polebridge, 1988.
_____. *The Formation of Q: Trajectories in Ancient Wisdom Collections*, Studies in Antiquity & Christianity. Philadelphia: Fortress Press, 1987.
_____, Marvin W. Meyer, Stephen J. Patterson, and Michael G. Steinhauser. *Q–Thomas Reader*. Sonoma, CA: Polebridge Press, 1990.
Kloppenborg, Verbin, John S. *Excavating Q: The History and Setting of the Sayings Gospel*. Minneapolis: Fortress, 2000.
Miller, Robert J., ed. *The Complete Gospels*. Sonoma, CA: Polebridge Press, 1992.
Patterson, Stephen J. *The Gospel of Thomas and Jesus*, Foundations and Facets Reference Series. Sonoma, CA: Polebridge Press, 1993.
Robinson, James M., ed. *The Nag Hammadi Library in English*. 2 ed. San Francisco: Harper and Row, 1977; 1988.
_____, Paul Hoffmann and John S. Kloppenborg. *The Critical Edition of Q*, Hermeneia. Minneapolis: Fortress Press, 2000.

Social science studies

Social science studies have had a great influence on recent New Testament scholarship, and one of the best books for an easy entrance into this field is Bruce Malina's *New Testament World*. Malina was not only one of the early pioneers in this field, but he has a gift for making the sometimes abstract material available to students at all levels. I have learned a lot from Bruce over the years. Malina and Richard L. Rohrbaugh's *Social-Science Commentary on the Synoptic Gospels* provide many helpful guides to a general reader from this perspective.

Malina, Bruce J. *The New Testament World, Insights from Cultural Anthropology*. Atlanta: John Knox, 1981.
_____. *The Social World of Jesus and the Gospels*. London and New York: Routledge, 1996.
_____. *Christian Origins and Cultural Anthropology: Practical Models for Biblical Interpretation*. Atlanta: John Knox, 1986.

_____, and Richard L. Rohrbaugh. *Social Science Commentary on the Synoptic Gospels*. Minneapolis: Fortress Press, 1992.

Leaven and mustard seed

The two most important articles on the parables of the Leaven and the Mustard seed are those of Robert Funk. He changed forever the way these two parables are understood and demonstrated a powerful new way of understanding parables as metaphor. The two are a wonderful read.

Funk, Robert W. *Jesus as Precursor, Semeia Supplements*. Philadelphia: Fortress Press, 1975. Reprint, Sonoma, CA: Polebridge Press, 1994.

Empty jar

My article was the first full scale scholarly effort to understand the parable.

Scott, Bernard Brandon. "The Empty Jar." *Forum* 3 (1987): 77–80.
_____. *Hear Then the Parable, a Commentary on the Parables of Jesus*. Minneapolis: Fortress Press, 1989, 306–08.

Treasure

By far the most important work on the parable of the Treasure is Dominic Crossan's monograph, *Finding is the First Act*. This work is important for several reasons. Crossan demonstrated the importance of knowing the options in telling a story, the various ways a theme has been played out in a tradition. Crossan made an all but exhaustive collection of treasure stories and showed that in such stories finding is not the first act. This has profound implications for how one interprets Jesus' story. Crossan also accented the problematic character of the man's action, something the tradition and most interpreters are anxious to avoid.

Crossan, John Dominic. *Finding is the First Act*. Semeia Supplements, Philadelphia: Fortress Press, 1979.

Samaritan

Again, Robert Funk's chapter on the Good Samaritan revolutionized the study of this parable.

Funk, Robert W. *Language, Hermeneutic and Word of God*. New York: Harper and Row, 1966, pp. 199–222.

Shrewd manager

Dan Via's treatment of this parable as a rogue story has always impressed me and I'm indebted to William Herzog's analysis of the messianic implications of the parable.

Herzog, William R. *Parables as Subversive Speech: Jesus as Pedagogue of the Oppressed*. Louisville: Westminster/John Knox, 1994.
Via, Dan. *The Parables: Their Literary and Existential Dimension*. Philadelphia: Fortress Press, 1967.

Unforgiving slave

Edward Beutner's essay "A Mercy Unextended" helped me to focus on what was going on in this parable. When he suggests as an equivalent contemporary opening, "A drug lord decides to settle accounts with his dealers" he caught the social situation and the dramatic effect on the audience perfectly. Beutner reminds us that we let the kings and masters off the hook far too easily.

William Herzog does much the same thing but in a much more technical way. Herzog has taken the parables as encoding of social oppression to a new and impressive level. I'm highly indebted to his work.

Beutner, Edward F. "A Mercy Unextended." *The Fourth R* 12, no. 5/6 (1999): 11–15.
Herzog, William R. III. *Parables as Subversive Speech: Jesus as Pedagogue of the Oppressed*.

Works Cited

The Babylonian Talmud. Edited by I. Epstein. 16 vols. London: Soncino Press, 1961.

Barrett, C.K. *The New Testament Background: Selected Documents*. New York: Harper and Row, 1956.

Bloom, Harold. *The Western Canon: The Books and School of the Ages*. New York: Harcourt Brace & Company, 1994, 51

Charlesworth, James H., ed. *The Old Testament Pseudepigrapha, 2 vols,*. Garden City, NY: Doubleday, 1983, 1985

Dodd, C.H. *The Parables of the Kingdom*. New York: Charles Scribner's Sons, 1935, 1961.

The Fathers According to Rabbi Nathan. Translated by Judah Goldin, *Yale Judaica Series*. New Haven: Yale University Press, 1955.

Franklin, R.W., ed. *The Poems of Emily Dickinson, a Reading Edition*. Cambridge: Belknap Press of Harvard University Press, 1999.

Funk, Robert W. *Jesus as Precursor, Semeia Supplements*. Philadelphia: Fortress Press, 1975; reprinted Sonoma, CA: Polebridge Press, 1994.

Funk, Robert W., Bernard Brandon Scott, and James R. Butts, eds. *The Parables of Jesus: Red Letter Edition*. Sonoma, CA: Polebridge Pess, 1988.

_____, Roy W. Hoover, and The Jesus Seminar, eds. *The Five Gospels: The Search for the Authentic Words of Jesus*. New York: Macmillan Publishing Company, 1993.

_____, and The Jesus Seminar, eds. *The Acts of Jesus: Search for the Authentic Deeds of Jesus*. San Francisco: HarperSanFrancisco, 1998.

Hammarskjöld, Dag. *Markings*, New York: Alfred A. Knopf, 1964.

Havel, Vaclav. *Disturbing the Peace*. London: Faber and Faber, 1990, 181.

Heaney, Seamus. *The Redress of Poetry*. London: Faber and Faber, 1995.

Jeremias, Joachim. *The Parables of Jesus*. Translated by S.H. Hooke. New York: Charles Scribner's Sons, 1972.

Josephus. *Complete Works*. Translated by William Whinton in numerous reprints.

Kafka, Franz. *Parables and Paradoxes*. New York: Schocken Books, 1935.

Lakoff, George, and Mark Johnson. Metaphors We Live By. Chicago: University of Chicago Press, 1980.

Lévi-Strauss, Claude. *The Raw and the Cooked: Introduction to a Science of Mythology*. Translated by John Weightman and Doreen Weightman. Vol. 1. New York: Harper and Row, 1969.

Loeb Classical Library. Cambridge: Harvard University Press; London: William Heineman.

Midrash on Psalms. Translated by William Braude. 2 vols. Yale Judaica Series. New Haven: Yale University Press, 1959.

Midrash Rabbah. Translated by H. Freedman and Maurice Simon, 10 vols. London: Soncino Press.

Miller, Robert J., ed. *The Complete Gospels*. Sonoma, CA: Polebridge Press, 1992.

The Mishnah. Translated by Herbert Danby. Oxford: At the Clarendon Press, 1933.

The Mishnah, a New Translation. Translated by Jacob Neusner. New Haven: Yale University Press, 1988.

Montefiore, Claude G., and H. Loewe, eds. *A Rabbinic Anthology*. Philadelphia / Cleveland: Jewish Publication Society of America. The World Publishing Company, 1960.

Montefiore, Claude G. *The Synoptic Gospels*. 2 ed. Vol. 1. New York: KTAV Publishing House, 1968.

Montefiore, Hugh, and H.Turner. *Thomas and the Evangelists*. Studies in Biblical Theology 35. Naperville, Ill.: Alec R. Allenson, 1962.

Ong, Walter J. *Orality and Literacy, the Technologizing of the Word*. Edited by Terence Hawkes, *New Accents*. London and New York: Methuen, 1982.

Scott, Bernard Brandon. *Hear Then the Parable, a Commentary on the Parables of Jesus*. Minneapolis: Fortress Press, 1989.

Stowers, Stanley K. *A Rereading of Romans: Justice, Jews, and Gentiles*. New Haven/London: Yale University Press, 1994.

The Talmud of the Land of Israel. Translated by Jacob Neusner. 35 vols. Chicago: University of Chicago Press, 1983-

Vermes, G. *The Dead Sea Scrolls in English*. 3rd ed. London: Penguin Books, 1987.

Index

CPSIA information can be obtained at www.ICGtesting.com
Printed in the USA
BVOW08s1331060215

386364BV00005B/18/P